I0020247

DISTRIBUTED CACHING & DATA MANAGEMENT

MASTERING REDIS, MEMCACHED, AND APACHE IGNITE CACHING

3 BOOKS IN 1

BOOK 1
MASTERING REDIS AND MEMCACHED FOR REAL-TIME DATA CACHING

BOOK 2
BUILDING SCALABLE DATA SYSTEMS WITH APACHE IGNITE

BOOK 3
ADVANCED CACHING TECHNIQUES: REDIS, MEMCACHED, AND APACHE IGNITE IN PRACTICE

ROB BOTWRIGHT

Copyright © 2025 by Rob Botwright
All rights reserved. No part of this book may be reproduced
or transmitted in any form or by any means, electronic or
mechanical, including photocopying, recording, or by any
information storage and retrieval system, without
permission in writing from the publisher.

Published by Rob Botwright
Library of Congress Cataloging-in-Publication Data
ISBN 978-1-83938-930-6
Cover design by Rizzo

Disclaimer

The contents of this book are based on extensive research and the best available historical sources. However, the author and publisher make no claims, promises, or guarantees about the accuracy, completeness, or adequacy of the information contained herein. The information in this book is provided on an "as is" basis, and the author and publisher disclaim any and all liability for any errors, omissions, or inaccuracies in the information or for any actions taken in reliance on such information. The opinions and views expressed in this book are those of the author and do not necessarily reflect the official policy or position of any organization or individual mentioned in this book. Any reference to specific people, places, or events is intended only to provide historical context and is not intended to defame or malign any group, individual, or entity. The information in this book is intended for educational and entertainment purposes only. It is not intended to be a substitute for professional advice or judgment. Readers are encouraged to conduct their own research and to seek professional advice where appropriate. Every effort has been made to obtain necessary permissions and acknowledgments for all images and other copyrighted material used in this book. Any errors or omissions in this regard are unintentional, and the author and publisher will correct them in future editions.

BOOK 1 - MASTERING REDIS AND MEMCACHED FOR REAL-TIME DATA CACHING

Introduction 5
Chapter 1: Introduction to Data Caching 7
Chapter 2: Understanding Redis: Architecture and Core Concepts 11
Chapter 3: Getting Started with Memcached 16
Chapter 4: Setting Up Redis and Memcached for Optimal Performance 21
Chapter 5: Data Structures in Redis: Keys, Strings, and More 26
Chapter 6: Advanced Redis Features: Pub/Sub and Persistence 31
Chapter 7: Scaling Your Cache: Redis Clustering and Memcached Sharding 36
Chapter 8: Cache Eviction Strategies: Managing Cache Size Efficiently 41
Chapter 9: Optimizing Performance: Tuning Redis and Memcached 45
Chapter 10: Integrating Redis and Memcached with Web Applications 50
Chapter 11: Real-World Use Cases: Caching for Web Apps and APIs 56
Chapter 12: Troubleshooting and Monitoring Cache Systems 61

BOOK 2 - BUILDING SCALABLE DATA SYSTEMS WITH APACHE IGNITE

Chapter 1: Introduction to Apache Ignite 67
Chapter 2: Setting Up Apache Ignite for High-Performance Data Systems 72
Chapter 3: Understanding Apache Ignite Architecture 78
Chapter 4: In-Memory Computing Fundamentals 83
Chapter 5: Data Grids and Caching in Apache Ignite 88
Chapter 6: Scaling with Apache Ignite Clustering 93
Chapter 7: Advanced Data Storage and Persistence in Ignite 98
Chapter 8: Ignite SQL and Querying for Real-Time Data 103
Chapter 9: Integrating Apache Ignite with Other Systems 109
Chapter 10: Performance Tuning and Optimization in Apache Ignite 114
Chapter 11: Building Fault-Tolerant and High-Availability Systems 119
Chapter 12: Real-World Use Cases: Apache Ignite in Action 125

BOOK 3 - ADVANCED CACHING TECHNIQUES: REDIS, MEMCACHED, AND APACHE IGNITE IN PRACTICE

Chapter 1: Introduction to Advanced Caching Techniques 132
Chapter 2: Deep Dive into Redis: Advanced Features and Use Cases 137
Chapter 3: Memcached Beyond the Basics: Performance and Scalability 143
Chapter 4: Apache Ignite: Leveraging In-Memory Data Grids for Caching 149
Chapter 5: Data Sharding and Partitioning in Distributed Caching Systems 154
Chapter 6: Managing Cache Eviction and Expiration Strategies 160
Chapter 7: Integrating Redis, Memcached, and Apache Ignite for Hybrid Caching Solutions 165
Chapter 8: Optimizing Cache Performance: Tuning Redis, Memcached, and Ignite 171
Chapter 9: Cache Synchronization and Consistency in Distributed Systems 177
Chapter 10: Real-Time Caching for High-Volume Applications 183
Chapter 11: Security and Fault Tolerance in Distributed Caching 188
Chapter 12: Monitoring, Troubleshooting, and Scaling Distributed Caching Systems 194
Conclusion 200

Introduction

In the rapidly evolving world of data management, achieving speed, scalability, and reliability has become more critical than ever. Distributed caching has emerged as one of the most effective ways to address these challenges, enabling systems to deliver high-performance data access while minimizing the load on primary databases. Whether you're building real-time applications, handling large datasets, or designing mission-critical systems, mastering distributed caching is essential for success. This book is a comprehensive guide to three of the most powerful caching technologies in use today: Redis, Memcached, and Apache Ignite. Across three books, we will explore these tools in-depth, starting with the fundamentals and advancing to more complex concepts and techniques. In **Book 1**, we will focus on Redis and Memcached, exploring how they can be leveraged for real-time data caching. **Book 2** will delve into Apache Ignite, a robust in-memory computing platform that enables scalable and highly available data systems. Finally, **Book 3** will tackle advanced caching techniques, showcasing how Redis, Memcached, and Apache Ignite can be used together to solve complex caching challenges in practice. By the end of this book, you will not only have a strong understanding of distributed caching concepts but also the practical skills to implement them effectively in your own systems. Whether you are a developer, system architect, or data engineer, the knowledge you'll gain here will be invaluable for building high-performance, scalable, and resilient data architectures that meet the demands of today's data-driven world. Let's dive into the world of distributed caching, unlock the full potential of Redis, Memcached, and Apache Ignite, and master the art of data management at scale!

BOOK 1

MASTERING REDIS AND MEMCACHED FOR REAL-TIME DATA CACHING

ROB BOTWRIGHT

Chapter 1: Introduction to Data Caching

Data caching is an essential technique used in computing to temporarily store data in a high-speed storage medium, such as memory, to facilitate faster access to that data. It is a method that optimizes the performance of systems by reducing the time needed to retrieve data from slower storage devices like hard drives or databases. Caching is fundamental to many applications and can significantly enhance the user experience by ensuring that data is available when needed, without having to repeatedly access the original source, which could be time-consuming and resource-intensive. The basic idea behind data caching is to store frequently accessed data in a faster, more efficient storage layer, reducing the number of expensive or slow read operations that the system needs to perform. For example, when a user requests data, instead of retrieving it from a distant database, the system first checks whether the data is already cached in memory. If it is, the data can be quickly retrieved, offering near-instant access. However, if the data is not cached, it is fetched from the slower data store, and then placed into the cache for future use. This creates a cycle of faster access to repeated data requests, improving both speed and efficiency.

There are different types of caching systems that serve various purposes, each providing specific advantages in particular contexts. In-memory caching, for instance, stores data in the system's RAM, providing extremely fast access. Systems like Redis and Memcached are popular for this use case, as they are designed to offer lightning-fast data retrieval with minimal latency. These systems are commonly used in scenarios where performance is critical, such as web applications and e-commerce platforms that require real-time access to frequently requested data. Caching is also an effective technique for improving the performance of databases. Many relational databases and NoSQL systems utilize caching mechanisms to store query results, database objects, or frequently accessed data to avoid repetitive and costly database queries. By storing the results of common queries in memory, caching reduces the need to perform the same operations over and over again, which can significantly alleviate the load on the database and improve overall system response times. Web applications often rely on caching to store static assets, such as images, JavaScript, and CSS files, in the browser's local storage. When a user visits a website, their browser will check the cache before making a request to the server, enabling faster loading times and reducing the need for repeated HTTP requests. Caching of static assets is crucial for improving the performance of websites, particularly when it comes to improving the user experience for large-scale websites with high traffic volumes.

Another key benefit of caching is that it reduces the strain on backend systems. When data is cached, the need to repeatedly fetch information from backend systems like databases, APIs, or file systems is minimized. This helps prevent bottlenecks in the system that can occur when too many requests are sent to these resources at the same time. For example, in high-traffic applications, such as social media platforms, caching plays a vital role in keeping systems responsive and efficient during peak usage times.

Caching can also be employed in distributed systems to ensure data consistency across multiple nodes. In such systems, caches can be maintained in multiple locations, ensuring that users and systems receive data from the nearest and most available cache, which reduces latency. Technologies like Content Delivery Networks (CDNs) use caching strategies to distribute web content across multiple servers worldwide, ensuring that users receive content from a server geographically closer to them, thus improving access speed and minimizing delay.

The effectiveness of caching depends on several factors, including cache size, eviction policies, and cache invalidation strategies. A cache's size must be carefully managed to balance between storing enough data for frequent access and ensuring that it doesn't consume too much system memory. One of the common challenges with caching is determining which data should be kept in the cache and for how long. This is where cache eviction policies come into play. These policies determine when and how old data should be removed from the cache to make room for new data. Several eviction strategies exist, such as Least Recently Used (LRU), Least Frequently Used (LFU), and First In, First Out (FIFO), each suited for different use cases based on how data is accessed and updated.

Cache invalidation is another critical concept in caching. It refers to the process of ensuring that stale or outdated data is removed from the cache and replaced with fresh, accurate data. Without proper invalidation, users may receive incorrect or outdated data, leading to errors and inconsistencies. Cache invalidation can occur in several ways, such as when the data in the cache expires after a certain period or when the underlying data source changes and triggers a cache refresh. One important consideration when implementing caching in a system is consistency. Caching can introduce the possibility of data inconsistency, especially in systems with multiple caches or where data is frequently updated. This can lead to issues where a cache holds outdated data while the original source of the data has been modified. To mitigate this, various strategies such as cache coherence protocols, versioning, and synchronization mechanisms are used to ensure that caches reflect the most up-to-date information. In modern computing, caching is not just confined to memory or disk systems. With the rise of cloud computing and microservices architectures, caching has evolved to meet the demands of distributed and cloud-based systems. Services like Amazon Web Services (AWS) and Google Cloud Platform (GCP) provide managed caching solutions, such as Amazon ElastiCache and Google Cloud Memorystore, that integrate seamlessly with cloud-based applications and distributed systems. These cloud caching services offer high scalability, automatic failover, and low-latency access to cached data, making them ideal for applications with high demand.

Caching is not a one-size-fits-all solution, and its effectiveness varies depending on the specific needs of the application. For applications where data freshness is critical, such as financial systems or live feeds, caching must be carefully tuned to avoid serving outdated information. On the other hand, for applications where speed is the primary concern, aggressive caching strategies can greatly improve responsiveness and performance. Understanding the nuances of caching and how to implement it effectively is essential for any developer looking to build high-performance, scalable systems.

Chapter 2: Understanding Redis: Architecture and Core Concepts

Redis is an advanced key-value store that operates in-memory, designed for speed and efficiency. It is often referred to as a **data structure server** because it allows you to manipulate different types of data structures such as strings, hashes, lists, sets, and sorted sets with a wide variety of commands. Redis is most commonly used as a caching solution, but it also supports a variety of use cases, including session storage, real-time analytics, message queuing, and as a primary database for applications that require low-latency access to data. Its unique architecture and the way it handles data are key to understanding why it is so fast and efficient for these tasks.

At its core, Redis operates by storing data in memory rather than on disk. This provides it with significant performance benefits over traditional databases, which are disk-based and rely on slower data retrieval. Redis takes advantage of the speed of RAM to allow operations like setting, getting, and deleting data to be performed in microseconds. Unlike traditional databases that perform disk I/O operations to read and write data, Redis stores all its data in memory, which is why it is capable of such high performance and low-latency responses.

The architecture of Redis is built around a single-threaded event loop, which processes multiple operations concurrently in a non-blocking manner. Despite being single-threaded, Redis can handle a high volume of operations per second. The reason Redis is so efficient is because it is built using an event-driven, non-blocking architecture, where the server listens to incoming commands, processes them, and returns a result in real time. This architecture is simple, yet effective, as it avoids the complexity of multi-threaded synchronization, which can often introduce overhead.

A fundamental concept of Redis is that it uses a **key-value store** model, where each piece of data is associated with a unique key. You can think of Redis as a giant dictionary where the keys are used to retrieve the associated values. The values in Redis can take many forms: strings, lists, sets, sorted sets, hashes, and bitmaps. Redis allows complex operations on these data types, making it incredibly versatile. For example, with Redis strings, you can store simple values such as integers or text. With Redis lists, you can manage ordered collections of items that support various operations like push, pop, and range queries.

One of the more advanced features of Redis is its **persistence mechanisms**, which allow it to store data on disk to survive restarts. While Redis is designed as an in-memory database, there are configurations that enable it to save snapshots of its dataset to disk, which can be used to recover data in the event of a failure. There are two main persistence strategies in Redis: **RDB snapshots** and **AOF (Append-Only File)**. RDB snapshots are taken periodically and represent a point-in-time backup of the entire dataset. AOF, on the other hand, logs every write operation received by the server, allowing you to reconstruct the dataset by replaying these commands. Both methods are configurable based on the application's needs for data durability and recovery time.

Redis is also highly **scalable** and can be distributed across multiple nodes to handle larger datasets and higher throughput. Redis supports a clustering model in which data is partitioned across multiple Redis instances, allowing horizontal scaling. This is achieved by dividing the dataset into different slots, each of which is handled by a specific Redis node in the cluster. Redis also provides support for replication, where data from a master node is copied to one or more replica nodes. This feature enables high availability and fault tolerance, ensuring that Redis can continue to operate even if one of its nodes fails.

Another key feature of Redis is its **pub/sub messaging system**, which allows clients to subscribe to channels and receive messages published to those channels. This is often used for real-time messaging systems, such as chat applications or notification systems, where clients need to receive updates in real time. Redis's pub/sub functionality is simple and efficient, allowing messages to be pushed to clients as soon as they are published. This system is also very fast because Redis's in-memory architecture eliminates the need for disk I/O operations, making it ideal for real-time applications.

Replication in Redis allows data to be mirrored across multiple servers, ensuring that the data is available even if one of the servers goes down. This setup is critical for applications requiring high availability and fault tolerance. Redis replication is asynchronous, meaning that the master node sends updates to the replica nodes, but it does not wait for them to confirm that the data has been written before continuing with the next operation. While this can improve performance, it can lead to some data loss if the master node crashes before replication is complete.

Redis commands are a key feature that distinguishes it from other data stores. Each data structure in Redis has a specific set of commands associated with it, allowing for fast and efficient data manipulation. For example, strings support commands like SET, GET, and INCR, while lists support commands like LPUSH, RPUSH, and LRANGE. Sets have their own commands, such as SADD, SREM, and SMEMBERS. Redis's command set is simple to learn and allows developers to easily manipulate data without the complexity of traditional SQL queries.

The simplicity and flexibility of Redis commands are part of the reason why Redis is so widely used for a variety of use cases. From **session storage** to **real-time analytics**, Redis is an excellent choice for developers looking for speed and reliability. Many organizations use Redis in production environments to handle high-throughput use cases like caching, queuing, and pub/sub messaging.

Data eviction policies are another important aspect of Redis's functionality. Since Redis operates primarily in memory, it is important to manage how data is removed when the cache reaches its memory limit. Redis offers several eviction policies, including **noeviction**, **allkeys-lru**, and **volatile-lru**, among others. These policies dictate how Redis should handle data when it runs out of memory, determining whether it evicts the least recently used (LRU) keys or whether it simply refuses to add more data until space is available.

Redis is also designed for **atomic operations**. This means that Redis guarantees the atomicity of operations on its data structures, ensuring that operations like incrementing a value or appending a string are performed safely, even in a multi-client environment. This feature makes Redis a reliable choice for applications requiring data consistency and correctness.

Redis's ability to handle high volumes of data and provide sub-millisecond response times makes it an indispensable tool in modern software development. Whether it is used for caching frequently accessed data, queuing tasks for background processing, or enabling real-time messaging, Redis's architecture is built to provide the performance and scalability required by today's applications. With its wide range of features, simple data model, and powerful commands, Redis continues to be a go-to solution for developers looking to improve the performance and scalability of their systems.

Chapter 3: Getting Started with Memcached

Memcached is a high-performance, distributed memory caching system designed to speed up dynamic web applications by reducing the load on databases and other data sources. It is an open-source project that allows developers to store data in memory, making it accessible with very low latency, as opposed to retrieving it from slower data storage systems like traditional disk-based databases. Memcached is commonly used in web applications to store session data, database query results, and other frequently accessed data to enhance performance and reduce latency.

At its core, Memcached is a simple key-value store that can hold various types of data such as strings, integers, or objects. It provides a way for applications to store and quickly retrieve data using a key as the reference point. The simplicity of Memcached makes it incredibly efficient and easy to integrate into web applications, allowing developers to focus on their application logic rather than spending time on the intricacies of data management.

Memcached operates in a distributed fashion, meaning that it can scale horizontally by adding more servers to the cache cluster. This allows for seamless growth as the volume of cached data increases or the traffic load on the application rises. As new nodes are added to the cluster, Memcached automatically redistributes data to ensure that each server holds a portion of the cache, providing greater capacity and fault tolerance.

The architecture of Memcached is straightforward, and it operates in a client-server model. The client sends requests to the Memcached server to store or retrieve data, and the server responds with the requested data. When a client makes a request, the server uses a hashing algorithm to determine which server in the cluster holds the relevant data, which helps distribute the cache evenly across the nodes in the cluster. Memcached can handle large volumes of concurrent requests, making it an ideal solution for high-traffic websites and applications.

Setting up Memcached is relatively simple. To get started, you need to install the Memcached server software on the server machines that will participate in the cache cluster. Memcached can run on Linux, Windows, and macOS, with most installations running on Linux-based systems for their performance and scalability. Once the server is installed, it is ready to accept client connections.

After setting up the Memcached server, you will need to configure your application to connect to it. Memcached typically communicates with the application using a simple TCP-based protocol, which is lightweight and fast. Various libraries and client APIs are available for most programming languages, including PHP, Python, Java, Ruby, and many others. These libraries abstract the communication with the Memcached server, making it easy to integrate the cache into your application without needing to deal with low-level network protocols directly.

The Memcached protocol supports a wide range of commands for interacting with the cache. Some of the most commonly used commands include SET, GET,

DELETE, INCR, and DECR. The SET command allows you to store data in the cache, associating it with a unique key. The GET command retrieves the data associated with a specific key, while DELETE removes the data from the cache. The INCR and DECR commands are used to increment or decrement numerical values stored in the cache.

Memcached also supports **time-to-live (TTL)** settings for cached data, which allows developers to define how long data should remain in the cache before it expires. This feature is useful for managing stale data and ensuring that cached content is kept fresh. The TTL value can be set when storing the data, and Memcached automatically removes expired data from the cache, freeing up space for new data.

One of the key advantages of Memcached is its ability to handle large amounts of data and traffic with minimal overhead. It stores data entirely in memory, allowing it to access and return cached data in milliseconds. This is a significant improvement over traditional disk-based databases, where data retrieval involves slower disk I/O operations. Since Memcached is memory-based, the access times are much faster, making it suitable for high-performance applications, real-time data processing, and large-scale web applications.

Memcached also supports **eviction policies**, which determine how data is removed from the cache when the memory limit is reached. Memcached follows a Least Recently Used (LRU) eviction policy by default, meaning that it will remove the least recently accessed data when new data needs to be stored. This ensures that the cache holds the most relevant and frequently accessed data while evicting older or less frequently accessed entries. The eviction policy can be adjusted to meet the specific needs of the application.

Another important concept in Memcached is **replication**. While Memcached itself does not support data replication out of the box, you can use third-party solutions or libraries to implement replication and high availability. In a typical deployment, Memcached is used in conjunction with other systems, such as databases or application servers, to provide a fully redundant and fault-tolerant system.

Memcached is often used in scenarios where data needs to be fetched quickly, but not necessarily stored permanently. For example, in a dynamic web application, queries to the database can be cached in Memcached to reduce the load on the database and improve response times. Other common use cases include caching session data, user preferences, configuration settings, and the results of expensive computations that don't change frequently.

One of the primary reasons Memcached is so popular is its ability to scale horizontally. As the demand for more cache storage increases, you can add more Memcached servers to the cluster, allowing it to handle larger amounts of data and higher traffic volumes. The process of adding new servers to the cluster is relatively seamless, and Memcached automatically redistributes the cached data across the available nodes.

However, there are some limitations to Memcached. Because it is an in-memory store, it is limited by the amount of available RAM on the servers. For very large datasets, this can become a constraint. Additionally, Memcached does not offer built-in persistence, meaning that data is lost when the server is restarted. This makes Memcached unsuitable for use cases where long-term storage and data durability are required.

In modern web applications, Memcached continues to be a go-to solution for improving performance and scalability. By reducing the load on databases and ensuring faster access to frequently accessed data, Memcached plays a crucial role in enhancing the overall performance and responsiveness of applications. Whether it's used for caching query results, session management, or as a distributed cache for large-scale applications, Memcached remains an essential tool in the developer's toolkit.

Chapter 4: Setting Up Redis and Memcached for Optimal Performance

Setting up Redis and Memcached for optimal performance requires careful consideration of the hardware, network configuration, and memory management to ensure that these caching systems deliver the best results for your application. Both Redis and Memcached are in-memory data stores, but they have different architectures and configurations that can affect performance. By properly configuring them and following best practices, you can maximize their speed and reliability, ensuring they meet the needs of high-traffic applications that require low-latency access to frequently accessed data.

The first step in setting up Redis and Memcached is ensuring that the hardware is properly configured. Since both systems rely heavily on memory, having sufficient RAM is crucial for achieving optimal performance. In a typical deployment, the available memory should be large enough to store all frequently accessed data without the need to rely on disk access. For Redis, it's important to ensure that the server has enough memory for the dataset and the persistence options you choose, such as RDB snapshots or AOF logging. Memcached, being a purely in-memory store, is also limited by the available system memory, so it's critical to allocate sufficient resources to handle your data size and traffic.

Another aspect of hardware configuration is the CPU and network. Redis is single-threaded by design, which means it can take full advantage of a single CPU core. However, the overall system performance can be enhanced by having multiple cores to handle the underlying operating system processes and network traffic. Memcached, on the other hand, can be multithreaded, allowing it to distribute the load across multiple CPU cores. This makes Memcached a better choice for systems that require high parallelism and can benefit from multi-core processors. For both systems, ensuring that the server's network interface has enough throughput is essential to prevent bottlenecks, especially when handling high volumes of requests from clients.

Once the hardware is set up, the next step is configuring the Redis or Memcached server to ensure they perform optimally under heavy loads. Both Redis and Memcached are designed to be lightweight and fast, but there are a few key configuration options that can have a significant impact on performance. For Redis, configuring the **maxmemory** setting is essential. This option determines the maximum amount of memory Redis is allowed to use, and it ensures that Redis will start evicting keys once the memory limit is reached. It's crucial to choose a value for **maxmemory** that reflects your available resources and expected workload, as using too much memory can lead to system instability or excessive swapping, which will degrade performance.

In addition to **maxmemory**, Redis offers several **eviction policies** that determine how it handles memory when it reaches its limit. Common eviction strategies include **LRU (Least Recently Used)**, **LFU (Least Frequently Used)**, and **TTL-based (Time-to-Live)** policies. Choosing the right eviction policy is important for ensuring that Redis maintains a high level of performance. For example, if your application frequently accesses the same data, an LRU or LFU eviction policy may be more effective than TTL-based evictions. In Memcached, eviction works in a similar way, with the default policy being LRU. You can tune this behavior using the **-M** option when running Memcached to manage the memory more efficiently, especially when using Memcached in multi-node configurations.

For both Redis and Memcached, **persistent storage** should be considered based on the application's requirements. While both Redis and Memcached are designed primarily as in-memory data stores, Redis supports persistence through the **RDB (Redis Database)** snapshots and **AOF (Append-Only File)** logging. If persistence is a priority for your application, it is important to configure Redis with an appropriate persistence strategy. Redis allows you to configure the frequency of RDB snapshots and the append-only file, which can impact performance. For example, saving RDB snapshots too frequently can slow down Redis, so you should find the right balance between data durability and performance.

On the other hand, Memcached does not support persistence natively, as it is designed to be a purely in-memory caching solution. If your application requires data persistence, Memcached might not be the best choice for long-term storage, and you may need to consider using other solutions like Redis or a traditional database. However, Memcached's simplicity and speed make it an excellent option for caching frequently requested data that doesn't need to be stored permanently.

When deploying Redis and Memcached in a production environment, **clustering** is an important consideration for scalability. Redis supports clustering, which allows it to distribute data across multiple nodes, increasing both memory capacity and performance. Redis clustering automatically partitions data and assigns it to different nodes, making it highly scalable and fault-tolerant. For optimal performance in a Redis cluster, it's important to carefully design the number of nodes and ensure that the data is evenly distributed across them. You can adjust the **hash slots** to optimize key distribution and reduce network latency.

Memcached also supports clustering through **consistent hashing**. In a Memcached cluster, the cache data is distributed among multiple nodes using a hash algorithm that ensures even distribution of keys. This allows Memcached to scale horizontally as you add more nodes, improving both the cache size and throughput. However, unlike Redis, Memcached's clustering is not as advanced and doesn't offer the same level of fault tolerance. If a node goes down in a Memcached cluster, the data that was stored in that node may be lost, unless you implement your own data replication and failover mechanisms.

Another key aspect of performance tuning is **monitoring**. Both Redis and Memcached offer various tools to monitor their performance in real-time. Redis provides the **MONITOR** command and a set of Redis commands for inspecting system metrics, such as memory usage, client connections, and command execution times. Memcached provides similar capabilities through the **stats** command, which gives detailed information about memory usage, eviction rates, and hit/miss ratios. Regular monitoring of these metrics is essential to identify performance bottlenecks, memory leaks, or other issues that may arise during operation.

For high-traffic applications, **load balancing** is another critical element in maintaining optimal performance. Both Redis and Memcached can be used with load balancers to distribute client requests across multiple cache nodes, ensuring that no single node is overwhelmed with traffic. This helps to prevent performance degradation and ensures that the cache remains responsive even under high loads. Additionally, it's important to configure **replication** for both systems, as it can provide higher availability and fault tolerance. Redis supports master-slave replication out of the box, while Memcached replication can be implemented through client-side logic or third-party tools.

Finally, **network latency** can have a significant impact on the performance of Redis and Memcached. To minimize latency, ensure that your Redis and Memcached servers are located as close as possible to the application servers that access them. Additionally, use **network optimizations** such as TCP_NODELAY to reduce the time spent waiting for packets to be acknowledged, thus speeding up data access.

With these configurations in place, both Redis and Memcached can be set up for optimal performance in production environments, allowing applications to scale efficiently while delivering low-latency data access. Proper tuning, monitoring, and scaling strategies are key to ensuring that these caching solutions operate effectively under varying loads and deliver the best possible results.

Chapter 5: Data Structures in Redis: Keys, Strings, and More

Redis is a powerful and versatile in-memory data structure store that allows developers to store and manipulate various types of data structures, making it a highly efficient tool for building scalable applications. At its core, Redis is a key-value store, but it offers a much broader range of capabilities through its support for a variety of complex data structures. Understanding how Redis handles these data structures—such as keys, strings, hashes, lists, sets, and sorted sets—is crucial for leveraging Redis effectively and achieving optimal performance in your applications. The foundation of Redis data structures is the simple yet powerful idea of keys and values, but what sets Redis apart is its ability to support a wide range of data types that allow developers to solve different kinds of problems with ease.

In Redis, every piece of data is associated with a unique key. The key serves as the identifier, and it can be used to store, retrieve, and manage the corresponding value. The key can be thought of as the index in a dictionary, and the value is the actual data being stored. While Redis is often used for simple key-value pairs, the true power of Redis lies in its ability to store and manipulate more complex data structures. Redis supports a variety of data types, and each data type has its own set of commands and use cases. The ability to store and manage these complex data types in memory is what makes Redis such an attractive option for developers looking to optimize their applications for speed and scalability.

The simplest and most common data type in Redis is the **string**. In Redis, a string is just a sequence of characters or binary data, and it is one of the most flexible data types. A Redis string can store anything from simple text to more complex objects, as Redis allows you to store strings of up to 512 MB in length. Strings are used for basic caching, session storage, and storing simple data values. Redis supports a wide array of commands for interacting with strings, including commands like SET to store a string value, GET to retrieve it, and INCR to increment a numeric string value. Additionally, Redis allows you to append data to an existing string with the APPEND command, making it useful for operations such as building up a log or message history.

While strings are versatile, Redis also provides more specialized data types that offer enhanced functionality for specific use cases. One such data type is the **hash**, which is ideal for storing objects that have multiple fields. A hash in Redis is a collection of key-value pairs, where each field is associated with a value, making it a perfect data structure for storing objects. For example, a hash might represent a user profile, with fields like name, email, and age mapped to their corresponding values. Redis provides commands such as HSET, HGET, and HDEL to add, retrieve, and delete fields from a hash. Additionally, Redis allows for operations like HINCRBY, which increments a numeric field within a hash. Hashes are widely used for cases where you need to store structured data in a way that is more efficient than storing separate keys for each attribute of the object.

Another powerful data type in Redis is the **list**. A Redis list is an ordered collection of elements that allows you to push and pop items from either the head or the tail. Lists in Redis are implemented as linked lists, and they support operations such as LPUSH, RPUSH, LPOP, and RPOP to insert and remove elements from the list. Lists are ideal for scenarios where you need to manage a queue or stack, as they allow you to efficiently manage the order of elements. Redis also provides commands like LRANGE, which allows you to retrieve a range of elements from the list. This makes lists an excellent choice for implementing features like task queues, message buffers, and event logs, where the order of the data is important.

Redis also supports the **set** data type, which is an unordered collection of unique elements. Sets are useful when you need to store a collection of items without duplicates, such as tracking unique visitors to a website or managing a list of active users. Redis provides commands like SADD, SREM, and SMEMBERS to add, remove, and retrieve elements from a set. Additionally, Redis offers powerful set operations such as SINTER, SUNION, and SDIFF, which allow you to perform set-based operations like intersection, union, and difference. These operations are extremely fast due to Redis's in-memory nature, making sets an excellent choice for use cases that require efficient membership testing or set manipulation.

For scenarios where the order of elements matters, Redis provides the **sorted set** data type. A sorted set is similar to a set in that it stores unique elements, but each element is associated with a score that determines its position in the sorted order. This allows for efficient ranking and sorting of elements based on their scores. Redis provides commands like ZADD, ZRANGE, and ZREM to add, retrieve, and remove elements from a sorted set. Additionally, Redis allows for range queries based on the score, such as retrieving the top N elements in the sorted set or retrieving elements within a specific score range. Sorted sets are commonly used for implementing leaderboards, ranking systems, and priority queues, where the order of elements is critical and needs to be maintained dynamically.

Redis also provides other data types and features, such as **bitmaps**, **hyperloglogs**, and **geospatial indexes**, which can be used for specialized use cases. Bitmaps are used for storing and manipulating binary data, while hyperloglogs provide an efficient way to estimate the cardinality of a set, making them useful for approximating unique counts in large datasets. Geospatial indexes allow you to store and query location-based data, enabling you to perform operations like finding the nearest location to a given point on the globe.

In addition to the core data structures, Redis supports **transactions** and **pipelining**, which allow you to execute multiple commands in an atomic and efficient manner. Redis transactions ensure that a series of commands are executed together as a single unit, and if any of the commands fail, the entire transaction can be rolled back. Pipelining allows you to send multiple commands to Redis without waiting for a response to each one, reducing the overhead of network round trips and improving performance.

The flexibility of Redis's data structures makes it suitable for a wide variety of applications, from simple caching and session management to more complex use cases like real-time analytics and event streaming. Understanding how Redis handles different data types and how to work with them efficiently is essential for developers looking to build high-performance applications that leverage Redis for speed and scalability. By utilizing the appropriate data structures for your specific use case, you can ensure that your Redis deployment is optimized for both performance and reliability.

Chapter 6: Advanced Redis Features: Pub/Sub and Persistence

Redis is a versatile in-memory data structure store that supports a wide variety of features and capabilities that make it suitable for a range of use cases beyond simple caching. Two advanced features of Redis that significantly extend its functionality are **Pub/Sub (Publish/Subscribe)** messaging and **persistence** options, which provide real-time communication between different parts of a system and allow Redis to store data in ways that can survive server restarts or crashes. These features are key to harnessing the full power of Redis, whether for event-driven architectures, real-time messaging systems, or ensuring data durability in high-performance applications.

The **Pub/Sub** feature in Redis allows for an asynchronous messaging pattern where publishers send messages to channels, and subscribers receive those messages in real-time. This pattern is particularly useful in systems that require decoupled communication between components. In Redis, the publisher sends a message to a channel, and any subscriber that has subscribed to that channel will receive the message. The beauty of Pub/Sub lies in its simplicity and speed, as it uses Redis's in-memory data structures to facilitate message delivery with minimal latency. Redis's Pub/Sub mechanism is often used in real-time applications, such as live chat systems, notifications, and event-driven architectures, where systems need to react to changes and communicate efficiently without relying on synchronous request-response mechanisms.

To implement Pub/Sub in Redis, a client connects to the Redis server and subscribes to one or more channels using the SUBSCRIBE command. Once a client is subscribed to a channel, it will start receiving messages published to that channel. Publishers can then use the PUBLISH command to send messages to the channels to which clients are subscribed. The messages can be simple strings or more complex objects that can be serialized into a string format. Redis guarantees that messages will be delivered to all active subscribers to a channel, and the subscribers receive the messages as soon as they are published.

One of the key advantages of Redis Pub/Sub is its low-latency, high-performance messaging capabilities. Because Redis is an in-memory system, it can deliver messages to subscribers almost instantaneously, which is ideal for applications that require real-time updates. Pub/Sub is also highly scalable, as Redis can handle thousands of subscribers and publish/subscribe operations with ease. This makes Redis a perfect fit for scenarios like messaging platforms, stock tickers, social media feeds, and even Internet of Things (IoT) applications, where data changes constantly and needs to be pushed to many subscribers at once.

However, Redis Pub/Sub has its limitations. One of the key challenges with Pub/Sub in Redis is that it does not provide message persistence. If a subscriber is not connected to Redis when a message is published, that subscriber will miss the message, as it is not stored by Redis for later retrieval. This makes Redis Pub/Sub suitable for use cases where the message's immediate delivery is more important than persistence. For systems that require message persistence, Redis offers other features like **list-based queues** or external systems like Kafka or RabbitMQ, which offer durable message queues.

Moving on to Redis's **persistence** features, one of the core advantages of Redis is that it is an in-memory data store, meaning all data is stored in memory for high-speed access. However, this also means that data could be lost if the Redis server crashes or is restarted. To mitigate this issue, Redis provides multiple persistence options that allow data to be saved to disk periodically or continuously, depending on the requirements of the application.

There are two main persistence mechanisms in Redis: **RDB snapshots** and **AOF (Append-Only File)** logging. Both of these methods are designed to provide data durability while maintaining Redis's high performance.

The **RDB (Redis Database)** snapshotting mechanism allows Redis to take snapshots of the dataset at specified intervals. These snapshots are stored as binary dump files (commonly called dump.rdb) on disk. Redis creates a snapshot of the entire dataset, including all keys and values, which can be used to restore the data after a crash. The frequency of snapshots can be configured in the Redis configuration file, allowing you to balance between data durability and performance. For example, you can configure Redis to take a snapshot every 5 minutes or after a certain number of write operations. While RDB snapshots are efficient in terms of disk space and provide fast recovery times, they are not suitable for scenarios where a high level of data durability is required, as data written between snapshots will be lost in the event of a crash.

On the other hand, **AOF (Append-Only File)** logging provides a more durable option for persistence. With AOF, Redis logs every write operation received by the server in a sequential log file (commonly called appendonly.aof). Every time a write command is executed, it is appended to the AOF file, allowing Redis to rebuild the dataset by replaying the log entries after a restart. AOF provides a higher level of data durability compared to RDB snapshots because it can be configured to log every write operation, or at a configurable interval. Redis offers three AOF persistence modes: **always**, **everysec**, and **no-appendfsync-on-rewrite**, allowing users to balance between durability and performance. The **always** mode writes to the AOF file after every operation, providing maximum durability at the cost of performance, while the **everysec** mode writes to the AOF file once per second, which is typically used in production environments to achieve a good balance between durability and performance.

A major advantage of AOF is that it provides better durability than RDB snapshots, especially in high-write environments. However, the AOF file can grow large over time as it stores all write operations. To manage the size of the AOF file, Redis provides an **AOF rewrite** process that compacts the AOF file by removing redundant or outdated commands, ensuring that it doesn't take up excessive disk space.

One important consideration when using Redis persistence is how to handle **data consistency**. Both RDB and AOF have their strengths and trade-offs, and the choice between the two largely depends on the application's needs. RDB is typically preferred when fast restarts and low-latency reads are crucial, and some data loss is acceptable. AOF is ideal when durability is more critical, and the application needs to minimize data loss, but with some performance trade-offs.

Redis also supports **Hybrid Persistence**, which allows you to use both RDB snapshots and AOF logging together. This provides the best of both worlds: periodic snapshots for fast recovery, combined with AOF for durability and minimal data loss.

By configuring Redis with the right persistence options and leveraging Pub/Sub for real-time messaging, developers can build highly available, low-latency systems that meet the needs of demanding applications, such as real-time analytics, event-driven architectures, and high-availability systems. These advanced features allow Redis to support a variety of use cases, from caching and session storage to real-time messaging and data persistence, making it a versatile tool for modern application architectures.

Chapter 7: Scaling Your Cache: Redis Clustering and Memcached Sharding

Scaling your cache is a critical component of managing high-traffic applications and ensuring that they remain responsive under heavy load. Both **Redis** and **Memcached** are widely used in caching architectures to improve application performance by reducing the time it takes to retrieve frequently accessed data. However, as the data size grows and traffic increases, a single instance of either Redis or Memcached might no longer suffice. This is where scaling strategies, such as **Redis Clustering** and **Memcached Sharding**, come into play, enabling horizontal scaling and enhancing the ability to handle large volumes of data and traffic efficiently.

Redis Clustering is a powerful feature that enables Redis to scale horizontally by distributing data across multiple Redis nodes in a cluster. Redis Cluster allows Redis to automatically partition data across multiple nodes and to handle both **data sharding** and **failover**. Each Redis node in a cluster is responsible for a portion of the dataset, which is determined by **hash slots**. Redis Cluster divides the entire keyspace into 16,384 hash slots, and each node in the cluster is responsible for a subset of these slots. When data is stored in Redis, the key is hashed using the **CRC16** algorithm, and the resulting hash determines which node in the cluster will store the key-value pair. This allows Redis to scale by adding more nodes to the cluster, with each new node taking on a portion of the hash slots and distributing the load.

One of the primary advantages of Redis Clustering is its **automatic data distribution**. As new nodes are added to the cluster, Redis automatically rebalances the data by redistributing the hash slots, ensuring that the data is evenly distributed across the available nodes. This enables Redis to handle more data and traffic without requiring manual intervention. Redis Clustering also supports **automatic failover**, meaning that if a node in the cluster fails, one of its replicas will be promoted to the primary role, and the cluster will continue to operate without interruption. This provides high availability and fault tolerance, which are critical for ensuring that your cache remains available even in the event of hardware failures.

While Redis Clustering is an excellent solution for scaling Redis horizontally, it does have some limitations. For example, Redis Cluster does not support **multi-key operations** across different hash slots, meaning that commands like **MGET** or **MSET** that involve multiple keys cannot span different nodes. This is because Redis Cluster uses hash slots to partition data, and multi-key operations that involve keys in different hash slots cannot be executed atomically. To work around this limitation, developers can design their applications to avoid multi-key operations or use Redis features like **hashes** and **sets** to store related data in a single key, reducing the need for multi-key operations.

Memcached Sharding is another technique used for scaling the cache horizontally, but it differs from Redis Clustering in that it relies on **consistent hashing** rather than automatic partitioning. In Memcached, sharding is done manually or using a third-party client library that distributes the data across multiple Memcached nodes. Consistent hashing is a technique that maps keys to a fixed number of slots, and each Memcached node is responsible for a subset of these slots. When a key is written to Memcached, the client computes the hash of the key and determines which node will store the data based on the hash value. The beauty of consistent hashing is that it allows for a smooth distribution of keys across nodes and minimizes the amount of data that needs to be moved when nodes are added or removed.

With Memcached sharding, the client is responsible for managing the distribution of data, which means that the application must know about all the nodes in the cluster and must handle the logic for determining which node to send each request to. This requires using a **client-side hash algorithm** to ensure that keys are distributed correctly across nodes. Popular Memcached client libraries like **libmemcached** and **Spymemcached** provide built-in support for consistent hashing and automatic sharding, allowing developers to easily implement horizontal scaling without having to manage the complexity of manual sharding.

One of the advantages of Memcached sharding is that it is relatively simple and lightweight. Since Memcached itself is designed to be a fast, in-memory cache, sharding can be done with minimal overhead. Additionally, because Memcached is often used as a key-value store with simple data types, such as strings and integers, there are fewer complexities in distributing the data compared to Redis. Memcached also supports a multi-threaded architecture, which allows it to make use of multiple CPU cores, further improving scalability and performance.

However, Memcached sharding does come with some challenges. Since Memcached does not have native support for **data replication** or **failover** like Redis Clustering, you need to implement these features manually if you require high availability. If a Memcached node goes down, the data stored on that node is lost unless the application has been designed to handle such failures, such as by relying on secondary storage or using a replication mechanism. Furthermore, the lack of automatic data rebalancing in Memcached means that if nodes are added or removed from the cluster, the client needs to be aware of the changes and redistribute the data accordingly. This can add complexity to the management of the cache, especially as the system scales.

Both Redis Clustering and Memcached Sharding provide mechanisms for **horizontal scaling**, which is essential for handling large amounts of data and high-traffic workloads. However, the choice between Redis Clustering and Memcached Sharding depends on the specific requirements of the application. Redis Clustering is better suited for use cases where high availability, automatic data distribution, and fault tolerance are important, as Redis offers built-in replication and failover. Additionally, Redis supports advanced data types and provides more functionality beyond simple key-value storage, making it suitable for more complex caching scenarios.

On the other hand, Memcached Sharding may be a better fit for simpler caching use cases where the focus is on speed and scalability, without the need for advanced data structures or persistent storage. Memcached is often used in environments where the data being cached is relatively static or can be easily recomputed, and where high throughput with low latency is the primary goal.

In both cases, scaling the cache by using Redis Clustering or Memcached Sharding involves a careful balance between performance, complexity, and data consistency. Both solutions are designed to handle the challenges of scaling, but the architecture and configuration choices must align with the needs of the application. Whether using Redis for advanced use cases or Memcached for fast, distributed caching, understanding how to properly scale the cache is crucial for building reliable and high-performing systems that can handle increased traffic and large volumes of data efficiently.

Chapter 8: Cache Eviction Strategies: Managing Cache Size Efficiently

Cache eviction strategies play a critical role in managing memory efficiently in caching systems like Redis and Memcached, as these systems are typically constrained by the available amount of memory. Caching is used to store frequently accessed data in memory, allowing quick retrieval and improving application performance by reducing the load on backend systems, such as databases. However, since memory is finite, caches must implement strategies to decide which data to evict when the cache reaches its capacity. This ensures that the most relevant and frequently used data remains in memory, while less useful or outdated data is discarded to make room for new data. Understanding the different cache eviction strategies is essential for maintaining the performance and reliability of a caching system, particularly in high-traffic environments where the data being cached is dynamic and constantly changing.

One of the most common and simple cache eviction strategies is **Least Recently Used (LRU)**. The LRU algorithm prioritizes keeping the most recently accessed data in the cache. When the cache reaches its memory limit, the least recently used items are evicted to free up space for new data. This works under the assumption that data that has been accessed recently is more likely to be accessed again soon, while data that hasn't been accessed in a while can be safely removed. In Redis, the LRU eviction strategy is one of the most commonly used and is the default behavior when memory limits are set. It works well for many applications because it ensures that the cache retains the most relevant and frequently used data, but it also has its limitations, especially when data access patterns are irregular.

Another eviction strategy is **Least Frequently Used (LFU)**. Unlike LRU, which focuses on recency of access, LFU targets the frequency of data access. The LFU algorithm evicts the items that have been accessed the least over a certain period of time. This strategy is useful in scenarios where some data is frequently used but may not have been accessed recently. LFU works well when the goal is to keep data that is most often requested, even if it hasn't been accessed in the most recent requests. However, LFU can be more complex to implement and maintain than LRU because it requires tracking the frequency of access over time, which can increase overhead. Redis also supports LFU eviction strategy, and it can be configured as a way to fine-tune cache performance based on the specific use case.

First In, First Out (FIFO) is another eviction strategy that follows the principle of removing the oldest data from the cache first. In a FIFO cache, the first item to enter the cache is the first to be evicted when space is needed. While simple and easy to understand, FIFO is not always efficient because it does not account for the frequency or recency of access. This means that even if an older item is still frequently accessed, it could be evicted, and newer but less useful data could remain in the cache. FIFO is typically used in scenarios where the exact access pattern of the data is less important, and simplicity is prioritized over optimization. In Redis and Memcached, FIFO is a less commonly used eviction strategy because it tends to perform suboptimally compared to LRU or LFU for dynamic data access patterns.

For caches where the goal is to ensure that only **the most relevant data** is retained, Redis provides the **volatile-lru**, **volatile-lfu**, and **volatile-ttl** eviction strategies. These strategies apply specifically to keys that have an expiration set. With **volatile-lru**, Redis will apply the LRU strategy to keys that have a TTL (Time-To-Live), evicting the least recently used of the expiring keys. Similarly, **volatile-lfu** applies the LFU strategy to keys with a TTL, keeping the most frequently accessed data. The **volatile-ttl** strategy evicts keys based on their expiration time, prioritizing evicting the ones closest to expiring. These specialized eviction policies are beneficial for caches where certain data is only relevant for a short period and where TTLs are an integral part of the caching design.

The **Random** eviction strategy is another approach, where Redis randomly selects keys to evict when the cache is full. This method is simple and may work well in scenarios where the access pattern of the cached data is unpredictable, and no eviction strategy seems to provide a significant advantage. While random eviction is straightforward to implement, it can lead to less efficient memory usage because it doesn't prioritize data that is frequently accessed or that has a higher likelihood of being used again. As a result, this strategy is not commonly used in high-performance applications, but it can be an option for use cases with less predictable or critical data access patterns.

Time-to-Live (TTL) is an eviction strategy that involves setting an expiration time for each cache entry. Once the data reaches the set expiration time, it is evicted from the cache. TTL is often used in scenarios where data is only relevant for a specific period, such as session information, authentication tokens, or rapidly changing data like weather or stock prices. This ensures that stale data does not remain in the cache, improving data freshness. Redis supports TTL through commands like EXPIRE, and you can set the TTL for individual keys to control how long they remain in the cache before they are evicted automatically. This strategy is ideal for caching data that has a predictable lifespan, but it requires careful management to avoid evicting data too soon or retaining it for too long. Choosing the right eviction strategy for your caching system depends on several factors, including the nature of the data, the size of the cache, and the traffic patterns of your application. If your application's data access patterns are relatively predictable and follow an LRU model, using the LRU eviction strategy will likely be the most efficient. On the other hand, if your data access patterns are more unpredictable or if some data needs to be evicted based on frequency, LFU might be the better option. If you're caching data with a known expiration time, TTL-based eviction strategies are highly effective for ensuring that expired data is removed automatically.

Properly tuning and configuring your eviction strategy can have a significant impact on the overall performance of your application, particularly for high-traffic systems that rely heavily on caching. Using the appropriate eviction strategy ensures that your cache is always filled with the most relevant data and that memory is used efficiently, helping to reduce latency and improve the responsiveness of your system. For Redis and Memcached, these strategies offer a wide range of options for managing cache size, evicting outdated data, and optimizing performance in a variety of use cases.

Chapter 9: Optimizing Performance: Tuning Redis and Memcached

Optimizing performance is essential when working with in-memory data stores like Redis and Memcached, especially when these systems are integral to the speed and scalability of applications. Both Redis and Memcached offer high-speed data storage by keeping data in memory, but to maximize their potential, it's crucial to understand how to properly tune and configure them. Fine-tuning the configuration parameters of both systems can make a significant difference in their efficiency, responsiveness, and ability to handle large volumes of data and traffic.

For **Redis**, the first step in optimizing performance is understanding memory usage. Redis is an in-memory store, meaning that all of its data must fit into the system's available RAM. Therefore, it's important to configure the maximum amount of memory Redis can use with the maxmemory directive in the configuration file. Setting this value ensures that Redis won't consume more memory than is available on the server, which could lead to swapping and degraded performance. When Redis reaches the memory limit, it will evict keys based on the eviction policy configured, such as LRU (Least Recently Used) or LFU (Least Frequently Used), depending on the needs of your application. Choosing the right eviction policy can have a significant impact on performance, especially in systems where data access patterns are unpredictable.

Another key parameter for optimizing Redis performance is **persistence configuration**. Redis supports two main persistence mechanisms: **RDB (Redis Database)** snapshots and **AOF (Append-Only File)** logging. RDB snapshots provide a way to periodically save the entire dataset to disk, while AOF logs every write operation for durability. However, both persistence mechanisms can introduce performance overhead, so it's important to tune them based on the needs of your application. For example, you can configure the frequency of RDB snapshots to control how often data is saved, balancing data durability with performance. AOF provides more durability but can slow down write-heavy applications, so adjusting the AOF configuration, such as using the everysec option for less frequent syncing, can help reduce the performance impact. If performance is your priority and some data loss is acceptable, you may opt to disable persistence entirely.

Network performance is another crucial area to optimize. Redis typically uses a single-threaded event loop to handle commands, which means that network latency can play a significant role in the overall performance of the system. Minimizing the distance between the Redis server and the application servers is important for reducing network latency. Additionally, Redis supports pipelining, a technique that allows clients to send multiple commands at once without waiting for a response to each one. This reduces the round-trip time and increases throughput. Properly tuning the number of commands sent in a single pipeline can improve the throughput without overwhelming the Redis server with too many simultaneous requests.

In **Memcached**, the first optimization consideration is memory allocation. Just like Redis, Memcached is also an in-memory store, so ensuring that the system has enough memory to store the data is critical. Memcached allows you to configure the memory allocated to it using the -m option during startup. The size of the memory allocation should be based on the amount of data you expect to store in the cache, keeping in mind that the size of the data objects should be small enough to fit within the available memory to avoid frequent evictions. When configuring Memcached for high performance, it is also essential to properly manage the **slab allocator**, which organizes memory into chunks of different sizes to prevent fragmentation. Memcached automatically uses a slab allocator to allocate memory for cached items, and tuning the slab sizes can help achieve better memory utilization and avoid performance degradation due to fragmentation.

Memcached also offers several tuning parameters that affect performance, such as the **number of threads** used for handling requests. Memcached is multi-threaded, which allows it to utilize multiple CPU cores. By default, Memcached uses a small number of threads, but for systems with a higher number of cores, increasing the number of threads can improve throughput and reduce latency. This can be done by configuring the -t option, specifying the number of worker threads. For heavily loaded environments, configuring the appropriate number of threads based on the system's CPU resources can significantly enhance performance.

Both Redis and Memcached support **compression** to reduce memory usage, which can be beneficial when storing large objects. Compression can help improve memory efficiency but may come at the cost of CPU performance. With Redis, the compression option allows you to store compressed objects, reducing memory usage while maintaining the performance of memory retrieval. However, it's important to consider the trade-off between compression and CPU load, especially when storing and retrieving large datasets. In Memcached, compression is also supported through client libraries, which automatically compress data before storing it in the cache and decompress it when retrieving. However, for Memcached, the compression ratio should be carefully evaluated since the CPU overhead of compressing and decompressing data can negatively impact performance in some cases.

For **high-availability** and **scalability**, Redis and Memcached offer clustering and sharding options. Redis Cluster is designed to distribute data across multiple nodes, providing horizontal scalability and fault tolerance. Redis Cluster automatically partitions the data into hash slots and assigns each slot to a different node, allowing Redis to scale out across multiple servers. Each Redis node is responsible for a subset of the data, and the cluster can automatically rebalance data when nodes are added or removed. Memcached, on the other hand, uses **consistent hashing** to shard data across multiple nodes. Consistent hashing helps distribute the data evenly across the cluster and ensures that data is still available even if nodes are added or removed. Both Redis Cluster and Memcached sharding require careful planning to ensure that the cache remains balanced and that the system scales effectively without overwhelming individual nodes.

Another factor to optimize in both Redis and Memcached is **connection management**. Both systems support multiple clients connecting simultaneously, and efficiently handling these connections is essential for optimal performance. Redis supports **connection pooling**, which allows clients to reuse existing connections rather than opening new ones for every request. This reduces the overhead of establishing new connections and improves response times. In Memcached, connection pooling can also help reduce the cost of establishing connections by allowing multiple threads to share a set of persistent connections. Properly managing connections and tuning the connection pool size can help improve the throughput of the system, especially when handling high levels of concurrent traffic.

Finally, performance monitoring is essential to identify bottlenecks and optimize system performance over time. Both Redis and Memcached provide robust monitoring tools that allow administrators to track memory usage, hit/miss ratios, evictions, and other critical metrics. Redis provides commands like INFO to get detailed information about the system's performance, including memory usage, command processing times, and network statistics. Memcached also offers the stats command, which provides insights into cache hit/miss ratios, memory usage, and other key performance metrics. Regular monitoring allows you to track performance trends, identify areas that require tuning, and ensure that both Redis and Memcached are operating efficiently at all times.

Optimizing Redis and Memcached for performance requires a comprehensive understanding of the system's configuration options, tuning parameters, and operational requirements. By carefully managing memory usage, persistence settings, network configuration, and cache size, you can significantly improve the performance of these in-memory data stores, ensuring they meet the needs of high-performance, scalable applications.

Chapter 10: Integrating Redis and Memcached with Web Applications

Integrating Redis and Memcached with web applications can significantly improve the performance and scalability of your system, providing fast data retrieval, reducing database load, and enhancing user experience. Redis and Memcached are both in-memory data stores, which means they store data in RAM instead of traditional disk-based databases. This allows for faster read and write operations, making them ideal for use cases that require real-time data access. In web applications, caching is a common strategy to handle frequently requested data, session management, and reduce the overhead of repeated database queries. By incorporating Redis or Memcached, web applications can process high volumes of requests with minimal latency, improving response times and the overall efficiency of the application.

To integrate Redis with a web application, you would typically start by setting up a Redis server that the application can connect to. Redis supports various programming languages through official and third-party client libraries. Whether you're using PHP, Python, JavaScript, Ruby, Java, or any other popular programming language, there are Redis clients available to facilitate communication between your web application and the Redis server. These clients provide simple interfaces to perform operations such as storing, retrieving, and deleting data from Redis, allowing you to integrate Redis seamlessly into your web application's backend.

One of the most common use cases for Redis in web applications is **session management**. Web applications often need to store user session data, such as authentication tokens or user preferences. By using Redis as a session store, applications can manage sessions efficiently, since Redis provides fast read and write operations that make it an excellent fit for storing temporary data. Redis supports **data expiration** through the EXPIRE command, which allows session data to automatically expire after a predefined time, reducing memory consumption and ensuring that stale session data is removed. This feature is particularly useful for applications with high traffic, where session data needs to be frequently accessed but shouldn't occupy memory indefinitely.

In addition to session management, Redis is commonly used for **caching** frequently accessed data, such as database query results, API responses, or generated HTML pages. When a user requests data that has been previously cached in Redis, the application can retrieve the data from Redis instead of querying the database, reducing latency and improving performance. For example, in an e-commerce website, product information or user shopping cart data can be cached in Redis, so that repeated requests for the same product data are served quickly, without the need to access the database every time. The caching mechanism can be easily integrated into the application code by checking the Redis cache before performing a database query and storing the result in the cache for future use.

Memcached, like Redis, is also widely used for caching purposes in web applications. Integrating Memcached into a web application follows a similar approach, where a Memcached server is set up and client libraries are used to interact with it. Memcached is often preferred for simpler caching scenarios, where you need to store and retrieve simple key-value pairs quickly. It is particularly effective when the cached data is relatively static and does not require advanced data structures, as Redis offers. Memcached's simplicity and focus on caching make it ideal for scenarios where you want to quickly offload data from your database and reduce load.

When integrating Memcached into web applications, it is crucial to configure the **memory size** of the Memcached instance to ensure that the data fits within memory without causing excessive eviction or data loss. Memcached uses an **LRU (Least Recently Used)** eviction policy, so when the memory limit is reached, the least recently used items will be evicted to make room for new data. Therefore, understanding the access patterns of your data and configuring Memcached to handle large amounts of data efficiently is essential for preventing cache misses and improving application performance.

Both Redis and Memcached can be deployed in distributed environments, allowing you to scale your cache as the application grows. In a **clustered Redis setup**, Redis automatically distributes the data across multiple nodes, ensuring that data is partitioned and replicated to handle increased load and provide high availability. Similarly, Memcached supports **sharding**, which distributes data across multiple Memcached instances.

When integrating these systems into web applications, it is important to handle **data partitioning** correctly and ensure that the application knows which cache node to query for the requested data. This is typically achieved through client-side hashing, which helps route requests to the correct server.

For web applications that need **real-time messaging**, Redis also provides the **Pub/Sub** feature, which allows different parts of the system to communicate with each other by publishing messages to channels and subscribing to those channels to receive updates. This is particularly useful in web applications that require real-time updates, such as chat applications, notification systems, or live feeds. For example, in a real-time chat application, Redis can be used to broadcast new messages to all subscribers (users) who are subscribed to a particular chat channel, ensuring that users receive messages instantly. The integration of Redis Pub/Sub into a web application is straightforward, using Redis client libraries to subscribe to channels and publish messages in response to user actions.

Another critical aspect of integrating Redis or Memcached with web applications is managing **cache invalidation**. Cache invalidation is the process of ensuring that the cache is updated when the underlying data changes. For example, if a user updates their profile information, the application should ensure that the updated profile data is reflected in the cache to avoid serving outdated information. In Redis, this can be done using commands like DEL to delete cached keys or setting a new value for the updated data. Memcached provides similar functionality through the DELETE command, allowing you to manually remove cached items when they become outdated. Additionally, both Redis and Memcached allow for time-based eviction with expiration policies, ensuring that cached data automatically expires after a predefined time.

When dealing with large-scale web applications, implementing **cache consistency** becomes increasingly important. While Redis and Memcached provide powerful caching solutions, they both rely on the application to handle scenarios where the cache may become inconsistent with the underlying data source. This requires implementing strategies to ensure that the cache and the database remain synchronized, such as cache invalidation strategies, write-through caching, and write-behind caching. For instance, in write-through caching, whenever data is updated in the database, it is simultaneously updated in the cache, ensuring that the cache always contains the most up-to-date information. This can be a more complex integration but ensures that your cache remains consistent with the data source.

In addition to the basic caching features, Redis provides several other advanced features that can be integrated into web applications to further enhance performance and scalability. These features include **sorted sets**, **hyperloglogs**, and **geospatial indexing**, which can be used for more complex use cases such as ranking, approximate counting, and location-based searches. By integrating these advanced features into web applications, you can solve more complex problems, such as implementing a leaderboard, estimating unique users, or performing geospatial searches, all while maintaining high performance.

Integrating Redis and Memcached into web applications provides a robust solution for improving speed, scalability, and real-time capabilities. By caching frequently accessed data, managing sessions, and using advanced features like Pub/Sub and geospatial indexes, these tools can significantly enhance the responsiveness of web applications. Properly configuring these systems, managing cache invalidation, and ensuring consistency between the cache and the underlying data source will ensure that the integration delivers maximum performance benefits.

Chapter 11: Real-World Use Cases: Caching for Web Apps and APIs

Caching is a critical technique for optimizing the performance of web applications and APIs, enabling faster data retrieval, reducing the load on databases, and improving the overall user experience. Web applications and APIs often face challenges when handling large volumes of traffic, and caching is one of the most effective solutions to address these challenges. By storing frequently accessed data in memory, caching allows web applications and APIs to serve requests faster without the need to constantly query databases or perform expensive computations. Redis and Memcached are among the most popular in-memory caching systems used for this purpose, and they are commonly integrated into web apps and APIs to achieve performance improvements.

One of the most common real-world use cases for caching in web applications is **session management**. Many web applications require users to log in and maintain a session across multiple pages or interactions. Storing session data in a database for every request can introduce significant overhead and slow down the application. Redis is often used for session management because it provides fast read and write operations and supports automatic expiration of session data. When a user logs in, the application can store their session data in Redis using a unique session ID as the key. The session data might include information such as authentication tokens, user preferences, or user-specific data that needs to persist across requests. Since Redis is an in-memory store, session data can be accessed almost instantly, resulting in faster login times and a more responsive experience for users. Additionally, Redis supports expiration for cached data, meaning session data can be automatically purged after a specified time, which helps manage memory usage and ensures that stale sessions are removed. Another significant use case for caching in web apps and APIs is **query result caching**. Web applications that rely heavily on databases often face performance bottlenecks when making repetitive queries to retrieve the same data. For example, consider an e-commerce website where product information is frequently requested by users. Rather than querying the database every time a user requests product details, the data can be cached in Redis or Memcached to minimize the load on the database and reduce the response time for subsequent requests. The first time a request is made for a particular product, the application queries the database and stores the result in the cache. On subsequent requests for the same product, the application retrieves the data from the cache instead of querying the database again. This significantly reduces the latency of responses and improves the user experience by ensuring that data is served quickly. Redis, with its fast data retrieval capabilities, is particularly well-suited for this kind of use case, where quick access to relatively static data can lead to major performance gains.

Caching is also useful for **API response caching**, especially in scenarios where API endpoints return data that doesn't change frequently. For example, an API that provides weather data might return similar information for a particular city throughout the day. Instead of querying an external weather service or a database for the same information repeatedly, the response can be cached in Redis or Memcached for a certain period. When subsequent requests for the same data are made, the API can quickly return the cached response, reducing the number of calls to the backend services and improving the overall response time of the API. In addition to improving performance, caching API responses can help reduce operational costs by lowering the number of requests made to external services or databases. Many modern APIs use caching headers such as Cache-Control to manage the lifetime of cached responses, and caching systems like Redis can be integrated to handle this efficiently.

Full-page caching is another powerful caching technique used in web applications. Full-page caching involves storing the entire rendered HTML of a page, making it instantly available to users without needing to regenerate the content each time the page is requested. This is particularly useful for websites with content that doesn't change frequently, such as blogs, news sites, or product catalogs. By caching the entire page in Redis or Memcached, web applications can serve the content much faster than dynamically generating it for every request. This technique is especially effective for high-traffic websites, as it minimizes the load on backend servers and databases. For example, an e-commerce site could cache product listing pages, category pages, or search results in Redis. When a user visits one of these pages, Redis returns the pre-rendered HTML, eliminating the need for time-consuming database queries and template rendering. To ensure that the cached page remains up to date, the cache can be invalidated when the underlying content changes, such as when new products are added or inventory levels are updated.

In modern web applications, **content delivery networks (CDNs)** are often used in conjunction with caching systems to serve static assets, such as images, JavaScript files, and CSS stylesheets. CDNs cache static content at edge servers distributed globally, ensuring that users receive content from the nearest server, reducing latency and improving load times. Redis and Memcached are frequently used for caching dynamic content, while CDNs handle the caching of static content. This combination provides an efficient solution for serving both dynamic and static content quickly to users worldwide. By caching dynamic data in Redis or Memcached and offloading static assets to CDNs, web applications can achieve significant performance improvements, especially for international users.

Cache invalidation is an important aspect of caching, and it plays a crucial role in maintaining data consistency. In web applications, data often changes due to user interactions or system updates, and cached data may become outdated. Cache invalidation refers to the process of ensuring that outdated or stale data is removed from the cache and replaced with fresh data. There are several strategies for cache invalidation, including time-based expiration, manual invalidation, and event-driven invalidation. For instance, in a content management system (CMS), when a user updates a blog post, the cache for that post can be invalidated, ensuring that subsequent requests fetch the updated content. Redis supports features such as **TTL (time-to-live)** and **key expiration** to handle automatic cache invalidation. Additionally, Redis supports **pub/sub** messaging, allowing other components of the application to subscribe to cache invalidation events and update the cache when necessary.

Rate limiting is another use case where caching is valuable, particularly for APIs. Web applications and APIs often need to impose rate limits on how many requests a user can make within a specified time period. Redis is commonly used to implement rate-limiting mechanisms, where a counter is stored in the cache for each user or IP address. Each time a request is made, Redis is used to increment the counter, and if the counter exceeds the allowed limit, the request is rejected. This is an efficient way to prevent abuse of the system, as Redis can handle thousands of rate-limiting requests per second with minimal latency.

Lastly, **caching for microservices** is becoming increasingly important as applications are broken down into smaller, more modular services. Each microservice may have its own caching layer, which can improve performance by reducing inter-service communication and database access. Redis and Memcached are commonly used to store data locally within microservices, allowing them to quickly access frequently used information without relying on external databases or APIs. This decentralized caching approach is highly efficient for large-scale applications that require rapid communication between microservices. By strategically caching data in each microservice, the overall performance of the system can be significantly improved, reducing the burden on databases and other shared resources.

In all these use cases, caching with Redis or Memcached can significantly enhance the performance of web applications and APIs by minimizing database queries, improving response times, and reducing system load. By implementing caching strategies such as session storage, query result caching, API response caching, and full-page caching, developers can ensure that their applications remain fast and responsive, even under heavy traffic.

Chapter 12: Troubleshooting and Monitoring Cache Systems

Troubleshooting and monitoring cache systems like Redis and Memcached are essential tasks for maintaining high-performance, reliable applications that rely on caching to improve speed and scalability. Caching systems, while providing numerous benefits such as reduced latency, improved database performance, and decreased load, can also introduce complexities that need to be addressed when things go wrong. Whether it's a cache miss, data inconsistency, or performance degradation, understanding how to diagnose and monitor your cache systems is crucial for ensuring their smooth operation. Effective troubleshooting and monitoring can help you identify bottlenecks, optimize cache performance, and ensure that your caching strategy continues to meet the needs of your application as it scales.

Monitoring cache systems starts with tracking key metrics that reflect the health and performance of the cache. Redis and Memcached, both being in-memory stores, offer different ways to gather and analyze metrics. One of the first metrics to monitor in a cache system is **memory usage**. Since both Redis and Memcached store data in RAM, it is essential to keep an eye on memory consumption. If the cache consumes more memory than available, it could lead to swapping, where the operating system writes parts of the cache data to disk. This significantly impacts performance, as disk I/O is much slower than memory access. Redis provides the INFO command, which can give detailed memory statistics, such as the used memory, memory fragmentation, and peak memory usage. Memcached also has the stats command, which provides memory usage statistics, including the current memory allocation and the number of items stored in the cache.

Another important metric is the **hit and miss ratio**. Cache hits refer to the number of times data is successfully retrieved from the cache, while cache misses occur when the requested data is not found in the cache, requiring a fetch from the backend data store. Monitoring the hit/miss ratio is crucial for understanding the effectiveness of the cache. A high hit ratio indicates that the cache is performing well and serving data quickly, while a low hit ratio may signal that your cache is underused, or your caching strategy may need improvement. Both Redis and Memcached provide commands like GET or MGET to measure cache hits, but they also offer built-in statistics. In Redis, you can use INFO stats to check the hit and miss ratios, while Memcached's stats command offers similar statistics, including get_hits, get_misses, and evictions.

Evictions occur when the cache reaches its memory limit and needs to remove items to free up space for new data. Monitoring evictions is essential, especially in high-traffic systems. Frequent evictions can indicate that the cache is too small for the volume of data being stored, and this can result in performance degradation as data is repeatedly evicted and reloaded. Redis and Memcached both support different eviction policies, such as LRU (Least Recently Used), LFU (Least Frequently Used), and random eviction strategies. You can monitor the number of evictions in Redis using the INFO stats command and in Memcached with the stats command. High eviction rates are often a sign that the cache is either not large enough, the eviction policy is not well-suited for the application, or the cache is not being populated with the most relevant data.

Latency monitoring is another critical aspect of cache troubleshooting. High latency can indicate issues such as network congestion, slow responses from the backend database, or inefficiencies in cache management. For both Redis and Memcached, latency can be measured using various tools, including built-in commands like MONITOR in Redis, which provides real-time information about each command received and processed, including its execution time. In Redis, you can also use the LATENCY command to get detailed latency statistics for different operations. Memcached also provides latency statistics through its stats timings command, which breaks down the time spent on various operations, such as setting or getting data. If your cache system is showing high latency, it may be necessary to tune the configuration settings, such as the number of worker threads in Memcached or optimizing the persistence settings in Redis. In addition to memory usage, evictions, and latency, it is important to monitor **persistence** when using Redis in production environments. Redis supports two persistence mechanisms: **RDB snapshots** and **AOF (Append-Only File)**. Monitoring the persistence of data in Redis is critical for ensuring that data is not lost during restarts or crashes. Redis provides several configuration options to control how frequently RDB snapshots are taken and how often AOF files are rewritten. Using the INFO persistence command in Redis, you can gather data on the last snapshot time, AOF rewrite status, and other persistence-related metrics. Memcached, unlike Redis, does not offer built-in persistence, so it requires a different approach to ensuring data durability, typically relying on external systems or manual intervention.

Disk I/O performance also plays a role in cache system troubleshooting, especially when Redis is configured for persistence. If Redis is writing data to disk too frequently, it can negatively impact performance. This issue can be addressed by tuning the persistence settings, such as increasing the interval between RDB snapshots or adjusting the AOF rewrite strategy to reduce disk I/O. In high-write environments, tuning Redis persistence is crucial to preventing disk contention and ensuring optimal performance. Memcached, being an in-memory cache, does not have this concern, but its reliance on RAM requires careful management of available memory to avoid disk swapping.

Error logs are another invaluable tool for troubleshooting cache systems. Redis and Memcached both provide detailed error logs that can help identify underlying issues. Redis logs errors related to memory allocation, network issues, and persistence, and they can be accessed through the Redis log file, which is configurable via the logfile setting. Memcached also logs errors to standard output or a log file, depending on how it is configured. Common issues found in error logs include memory allocation failures, high eviction rates, and misconfigurations that could lead to performance bottlenecks. Regularly reviewing these logs can help proactively identify issues before they affect the performance of your cache system.

In addition to internal monitoring tools, you can use **external monitoring solutions** to gain deeper insights into the performance of Redis and Memcached. Tools like **Prometheus**, **Grafana**, and **Datadog** allow you to monitor Redis and Memcached performance in real-time by collecting metrics and visualizing them through dashboards.

These tools provide easy-to-understand graphs and alerts based on thresholds, helping you detect anomalies quickly and take corrective action before performance is impacted. For example, you can set up alerts for high memory usage, increased evictions, or degraded hit/miss ratios. Integrating these external tools with your cache system allows you to gain a more comprehensive view of system health and performance.

In environments where Redis or Memcached are part of a larger distributed system, **distributed tracing** tools like **Zipkin** or **Jaeger** can help you troubleshoot performance issues by tracing requests through multiple services and identifying where bottlenecks may occur. By integrating these tracing tools with your cache system, you can track how data is being accessed from the cache and identify any delays or failures in the caching process.

Effective troubleshooting and monitoring of cache systems require a combination of real-time metrics, configuration tuning, and proactive alerting. By monitoring key performance indicators such as memory usage, eviction rates, hit/miss ratios, and latency, you can ensure that your caching system performs optimally. Troubleshooting issues related to disk I/O, persistence, and network performance is also crucial to maintaining the reliability and speed of your cache. With the right tools and strategies in place, you can keep your Redis or Memcached cache running smoothly, ensuring that your web application or API performs at its best even under heavy load.

BOOK 2

BUILDING SCALABLE DATA SYSTEMS WITH APACHE IGNITE

ROB BOTWRIGHT

Chapter 1: Introduction to Apache Ignite

Apache Ignite is an open-source, distributed in-memory computing platform designed to accelerate data processing for high-performance, real-time applications. It is a highly scalable and fault-tolerant system that combines **in-memory data grid** (IMDG) capabilities with an integrated **distributed SQL database** and **advanced computation** capabilities. Apache Ignite provides powerful features such as **distributed caching, real-time analytics, ACID-compliant transactions**, and **machine learning**. It is well-suited for both small and large-scale enterprise applications that require high-speed data processing, real-time decision-making, and seamless scalability. One of the core strengths of Apache Ignite is its ability to handle massive amounts of data across distributed clusters while maintaining low-latency access to that data.

At the heart of Apache Ignite is its **in-memory data grid**, which allows data to be stored in memory across a distributed set of nodes in a cluster. This design significantly improves performance by reducing the latency associated with traditional disk-based data storage. Data stored in an in-memory grid is readily accessible by multiple nodes in the cluster, enabling high throughput and low-latency processing. Unlike traditional databases that rely on disk I/O, which can become a bottleneck in high-demand environments, Ignite's in-memory architecture provides sub-millisecond data access speeds, which is critical for time-sensitive applications such as financial services, e-commerce, and real-time analytics.

Ignite's architecture is based on a **distributed computing model**. Each node in the cluster can perform data processing, and the data is partitioned and distributed across the nodes, allowing for parallel processing of requests. The system supports **horizontal scalability**, meaning that as demand grows, you can simply add more nodes to the cluster to increase capacity and processing power. Apache Ignite provides a **dynamic partitioning mechanism** that automatically rebalances data across the nodes as the cluster grows or shrinks. This ensures that the data is distributed evenly, and each node can handle a fair share of the workload. Ignite also offers **fault tolerance** by replicating data across multiple nodes. If a node fails, another node with a replica of the data can take over, ensuring that the system remains operational even in the event of hardware failures.

One of Apache Ignite's most important features is its **distributed SQL database** capabilities. Ignite allows users to run SQL queries directly on data stored in memory across the cluster. Unlike traditional relational databases that store data on disk and rely on complex query execution engines, Apache Ignite uses **distributed SQL processing** to execute queries on data that is spread across multiple nodes. This approach provides significant performance advantages, especially when working with large datasets that are too large to fit on a single machine. Apache Ignite supports standard SQL syntax, which allows developers to run complex queries without needing to learn a new query language. It also supports **ACID-**

compliant transactions, which ensure that operations on data are consistent, reliable, and meet the requirements of real-time applications.

Apache Ignite also provides **advanced computation capabilities**. It includes a **distributed computation framework** that allows developers to execute computations across the cluster in parallel. This is useful for scenarios such as machine learning, graph processing, and other types of data-intensive analytics. With Ignite, computations can be performed on data that resides in memory, significantly speeding up processing times compared to traditional disk-based systems. Apache Ignite also supports **in-memory machine learning**, providing tools for building and training machine learning models directly in the memory grid. This allows for real-time, low-latency predictive analytics on large datasets, making Ignite an ideal choice for applications that require machine learning at scale.

One of the distinguishing features of Apache Ignite is its **distributed caching** capabilities. It can be used as a distributed, fault-tolerant cache to accelerate access to frequently accessed data in large-scale applications. Redis and Memcached are often used for caching in single-node or small-scale environments, but Apache Ignite takes this concept further by enabling caching across a distributed set of nodes, allowing for high availability and performance in large applications. Ignite's caching layer is highly customizable, supporting various caching strategies, such as **replication**, **partitioned caching**, and **near caching**, depending on the needs of the application. **Near caching** allows data to be cached on the local node to reduce the number of remote calls, improving performance for frequently accessed data.

Another key feature of Apache Ignite is its **integration with other big data tools**. Ignite can be integrated with systems like **Hadoop**, **Spark**, and **Kafka** to provide a powerful, unified platform for big data processing. Apache Ignite can act as a fast in-memory layer that accelerates the processing of data in these big data frameworks. For example, when combined with Apache Spark, Ignite can store the intermediate results of computations in memory, allowing Spark jobs to be processed much faster. Similarly, when integrated with Apache Kafka, Ignite can act as a real-time data processing engine that ingests streaming data and performs analytics on it in-memory, allowing for quick responses to changes in data. For **cloud-native environments**, Apache Ignite also supports **cloud deployment models**, making it an ideal choice for organizations building and deploying applications in the cloud. Ignite can be deployed on cloud services such as Amazon Web Services (AWS) and Microsoft Azure, providing scalable and fault-tolerant in-memory storage for applications running in the cloud. The ability to easily scale Ignite clusters in the cloud makes it a powerful tool for applications that need to dynamically adjust to varying loads and data volumes. Apache Ignite also supports integration with containerization platforms such as Kubernetes, which makes it easy to deploy and manage Ignite clusters in containerized environments.

In terms of **data consistency**, Apache Ignite offers a **strong consistency model** based on the **two-phase commit protocol** for transactional operations. This ensures that operations on data are consistent across all nodes in the cluster. The **atomicity** of transactions is guaranteed, meaning that either all operations in a transaction will succeed, or none of them will be applied, which is critical for applications where data integrity is essential. Ignite supports **distributed transactions**, allowing for ACID-compliant operations across a distributed set of nodes, which ensures data reliability and consistency even in complex, multi-node environments.

Apache Ignite also includes **security features** such as **encryption**, **authentication**, and **authorization**, making it suitable for use in secure, enterprise-grade applications. Data can be encrypted both at rest and in transit, providing protection for sensitive information. Additionally, Ignite supports integration with enterprise authentication systems, allowing for fine-grained access control over who can read or write data in the system.

With its combination of in-memory data grid capabilities, distributed SQL database, advanced computation features, and high scalability, Apache Ignite provides a robust solution for organizations seeking to build high-performance, real-time applications. Whether you're looking to optimize data processing, accelerate analytics, or manage large-scale caching, Apache Ignite offers a versatile platform capable of handling a wide range of use cases. Its ability to support horizontal scalability, fault tolerance, and low-latency processing makes it an ideal choice for building modern applications that demand high performance and reliability.

Chapter 2: Setting Up Apache Ignite for High-Performance Data Systems

Setting up Apache Ignite for high-performance data systems involves configuring the system to take full advantage of its distributed, in-memory computing architecture. Apache Ignite is designed to handle large-scale, real-time data processing with low-latency access, and setting it up correctly is essential to harness its full potential. This process involves understanding and configuring various aspects of the system, such as **cluster setup**, **data partitioning**, **memory configuration**, **persistence mechanisms**, and **high availability**, all of which contribute to the performance of the data system. Apache Ignite is particularly well-suited for high-performance systems, whether you are using it for real-time analytics, caching, or in-memory processing of large datasets. By understanding the key components and steps involved in setting up Apache Ignite, you can optimize it for the unique requirements of your application.

The first step in setting up Apache Ignite is the **installation and cluster setup**. Apache Ignite operates in a distributed environment, with each node in the cluster responsible for storing and processing data. To start, you need to install Apache Ignite on the nodes that will form the cluster. Apache Ignite can be installed on-premises or in the cloud, depending on your deployment requirements. Installation can be done by downloading the pre-built binaries from the Apache Ignite website or by building it from source. After installation, you can configure the Ignite nodes to form a cluster. Each node in the cluster should have a unique configuration, and you need to ensure that the nodes can communicate with each other over the network. This is typically done by configuring the **TCP discovery protocol** in the Ignite configuration file, which enables nodes to discover each other automatically and join the cluster.

Once the nodes are configured to communicate, the next step is to configure **data partitioning**. Apache Ignite uses a **partitioned data model**, where data is split across the cluster into **partitions**. Each partition is stored on a node, and the data is distributed based on a **hashing mechanism** that ensures data is evenly distributed across the cluster. The partitioning strategy is a key factor in the system's performance, as it dictates how data is stored and accessed. Ignite provides several configuration options for controlling the number of partitions, such as the **ignite.cache.partitionCount** setting, which determines how many partitions each cache will have. Proper partitioning ensures that data is distributed evenly across the nodes, allowing for better load balancing and parallel processing.

Another critical aspect of setting up Apache Ignite for high performance is **memory configuration**. Apache Ignite is an in-memory computing platform, which means that data is stored primarily in **RAM** for fast access. By configuring memory correctly, you can ensure that the cache and data grids have enough resources to store and process the required datasets efficiently. Apache Ignite allows you to configure the amount of memory allocated for **data storage**, **off-heap memory**, and **persistent storage**. Off-heap memory is used to store data outside of the Java heap, preventing garbage collection pauses and improving the system's ability to handle large datasets. When configuring memory for Apache Ignite, you need to consider factors such as the size of your dataset, the number of nodes in your cluster, and the memory available on each node.

For systems requiring persistence, Apache Ignite provides two main persistence mechanisms: **RDB snapshots** and **AOF logging**. Persistence in Apache Ignite ensures that data can be recovered in case of node failure or system restart. **RDB snapshots** periodically save the entire dataset to disk, allowing you to recover the state of the system after a restart. You can configure the frequency of RDB snapshots through the IgniteConfiguration settings. **AOF (Append-Only File)** logging, on the other hand, logs every write operation to disk, providing a more durable option for data persistence. AOF logging ensures that no data is lost even if the system crashes between snapshots. Depending on your use case, you can choose to enable or disable persistence based on the requirements for durability and recovery time.

High availability and **fault tolerance** are essential considerations when setting up Apache Ignite for high-performance systems. To ensure that data is not lost in the event of a node failure, Ignite supports **data replication**. Data replication involves creating copies of data on multiple nodes in the cluster, ensuring that if one node fails, another node with a replica of the data can take over. You can configure replication in Ignite by setting the replicaCount parameter, which defines how many copies of each partition should be stored. Replication is crucial for applications that require high availability and reliability, as it ensures that the system can continue operating even if a node fails.

Cache configuration is another key aspect of setting up Apache Ignite for high performance. Apache Ignite uses **caches** to store data, and you can configure these caches to optimize data access. You can define cache modes such as **PARTITIONED** or **REPLICATED** depending on your data distribution and redundancy requirements. In a **PARTITIONED** cache, data is distributed across the cluster based on partitions, while in a **REPLICATED** cache, each node stores a copy of the data. Choosing the appropriate cache mode is important for optimizing performance, as **REPLICATED** caches provide higher availability but are not as scalable as **PARTITIONED** caches.

In addition to partitioning and replication, **query processing** can also be configured to improve the performance of your Ignite setup. Apache Ignite supports **SQL queries**, allowing you to interact with your distributed data in a familiar way. To optimize query performance, you can use **indexed queries** by creating indexes on specific fields. This allows Ignite to execute SQL queries much faster by reducing the need for full table scans. You can create indexes on **key columns**, **fields** in **SQL tables**, and even **joins** to improve the performance of complex queries. Properly indexing your data can significantly speed up the retrieval of information from large datasets.

Apache Ignite also provides support for **compute grid** and **collocated processing**, which enables distributed execution of computations on the data stored in the cache. This allows you to run operations such as **map-reduce**, **machine learning**, and **graph processing** across the nodes in the cluster. By collocating the computation with the data, Apache Ignite eliminates the need to move large amounts of data across the network, improving performance and reducing latency. You can configure compute tasks and jobs to run on specific nodes, ensuring that data processing is done efficiently and at scale.

For real-time data processing, Apache Ignite supports **streaming analytics**. You can configure Ignite to ingest and process real-time data streams, such as logs, sensor data, or financial transactions. Apache Ignite allows you to create **continuous queries** that run in the background and automatically process data as it arrives. This is particularly useful for applications that require real-time analytics, such as fraud detection, stock trading, and IoT applications. Ignite's streaming capabilities are designed to handle high-throughput data with low latency, ensuring that your data processing remains fast and efficient.

Finally, **security** is an important consideration when setting up Apache Ignite. Apache Ignite offers built-in support for **authentication** and **authorization**, ensuring that only authorized users can access and modify the data stored in the system. You can configure **role-based access control** (RBAC) to restrict access to specific caches, operations, or compute tasks based on user roles. Additionally, Ignite supports **encryption** to secure data both at rest and in transit, providing protection for sensitive data. By configuring Ignite's security settings, you can ensure that your high-performance data system is both fast and secure.

Setting up Apache Ignite for high-performance data systems involves configuring the cluster, partitioning data, tuning memory usage, enabling persistence, ensuring high availability, and optimizing for real-time processing and query performance. By carefully configuring these elements, you can create a distributed, in-memory computing platform that meets the needs of high-demand, mission-critical applications. Whether you're building a real-time analytics system, a distributed cache, or a complex data processing pipeline, Apache Ignite provides the tools and scalability needed to deliver high performance at scale.

Apache Ignite is a powerful, distributed in-memory computing platform that provides high-performance, low-latency data processing and storage for large-scale applications. The architecture of Apache Ignite is designed to be highly scalable, fault-tolerant, and flexible, making it suitable for a wide range of use cases, from simple caching to complex real-time analytics. At its core, Apache Ignite is built around the concept of an in-memory data grid (IMDG), but its architecture goes beyond that, offering advanced features like distributed SQL queries, machine learning, and real-time stream processing. To understand how Apache Ignite works, it is essential to break down its architecture into several key components that work together to deliver high-performance, distributed data processing.

One of the foundational components of Apache Ignite's architecture is the **Ignite cluster**. An Ignite cluster is a collection of nodes (servers or machines) that work together to store and process data. Each node in the cluster is responsible for a subset of the data, and these nodes communicate with each other to ensure that the system operates as a single, unified platform. The nodes in an Ignite cluster are typically categorized into two types: **data nodes** and **client nodes**. Data nodes are responsible for storing and processing data, while client nodes connect to the cluster to perform operations like querying or inserting data. Client nodes do not store data but interact with the cluster through the network to access and manipulate data.

At the heart of the Ignite cluster is the **distributed data grid**. This grid stores the data across multiple nodes in the cluster, leveraging the memory of each node to provide fast, low-latency access to the stored data. Apache Ignite uses a **partitioned** approach to distribute data across the cluster. The dataset is divided into partitions, and each partition is stored on one or more nodes. When a node is added to the cluster, data is automatically rebalanced across the nodes to ensure that the partitions are distributed evenly. This partitioning model enables horizontal scalability, allowing the system to handle larger datasets and increasing workloads by simply adding more nodes to the cluster.

The **partitioning mechanism** in Ignite is based on a concept called **affinity**. Each key in the data grid is assigned to a specific partition using a hash function. The affinity ensures that all related data (keys) are stored together on the same node, reducing the need for cross-node communication during data access. This is especially important for performance, as it allows data to be accessed locally on a node without the overhead of remote calls. In addition, Ignite supports **collocated processing**, which means that computational tasks can be executed directly on the nodes where the data resides, avoiding the need to transfer large amounts of data across the network.

A critical feature of Apache Ignite is its **distributed caching** capabilities. Ignite provides a distributed cache where data can be stored across multiple nodes in the cluster for faster access. This cache can be configured in several ways, such as **partitioned caching** or **replicated caching**. In **partitioned caching**, the cache is split into multiple partitions, and each node in the cluster holds a subset of these partitions. This allows the cache to scale horizontally by distributing the data across the cluster. In **replicated caching**, a copy of the data is stored on each node in the cluster, providing higher availability and fault tolerance. Both partitioned and replicated caching strategies can be chosen depending on the application's need for data availability and redundancy.

Apache Ignite also provides **SQL querying** capabilities, which are essential for interacting with the data in a distributed environment. Ignite supports **distributed SQL** queries, enabling users to run SQL commands across the entire cluster as if they were working with a single relational database. This is possible because Apache Ignite supports an **SQL engine** that can execute queries across distributed data, handle joins, and support other relational database features. The SQL engine is integrated with the Ignite data grid, so the results of SQL queries are returned quickly and efficiently by directly accessing the in-memory data. Ignite supports standard SQL syntax, making it easier for developers who are familiar with relational databases to interact with distributed data in the Ignite platform.

To ensure **fault tolerance** and **high availability**, Apache Ignite uses **data replication**. Data replication allows Ignite to create copies of data across multiple nodes in the cluster, so if one node fails, the data can still be accessed from another node. Ignite uses **replicated caches** or **replica partitions** to achieve this fault tolerance. For example, in a replicated cache, every node in the cluster holds a copy of the data, ensuring that even if a node goes down, the data is still available from other nodes. For partitioned caches, Ignite maintains **backup copies** of each partition on one or more nodes. If the primary node for a partition fails, the backup node takes over, ensuring data availability and system resilience.

Another important component of Apache Ignite's architecture is its **compute grid**. The compute grid allows users to perform distributed computations across the nodes in the cluster. This feature is used for running tasks like **map-reduce**, **machine learning**, and **graph processing** on the distributed data in real-time. The compute grid enables developers to run computations on the data without having to move the data across the network, which improves performance and reduces latency. Tasks can be executed either on a single node or distributed across the entire cluster, depending on the size of the computation and the data involved. Ignite provides APIs for defining and executing compute tasks, allowing for flexibility and scalability when processing large datasets.

In addition to the core components, Apache Ignite provides **integrations with big data tools** such as **Hadoop**, **Spark**, and **Kafka**, enabling it to serve as a fast in-memory layer that accelerates the processing of data. Ignite integrates with Hadoop to speed up data processing by storing intermediate results in memory, which is much faster than writing to disk. With Apache Spark, Ignite provides a distributed in-memory storage system for

Spark's RDDs (Resilient Distributed Datasets), allowing Spark jobs to be executed much faster. When integrated with Kafka, Ignite can consume streaming data and process it in real-time, making it ideal for applications that need to ingest and analyze data as it arrives.

The **security** architecture in Apache Ignite is also an essential part of its design. Ignite offers features like **authentication**, **authorization**, **encryption**, and **auditing** to ensure that data is secure both at rest and in transit. Ignite can be integrated with enterprise security systems, allowing you to enforce role-based access controls (RBAC) and limit access to sensitive data. The system also supports **data encryption** for secure communication between nodes, as well as for encrypting data stored in the cluster.

Apache Ignite's architecture is designed to provide high performance, scalability, and fault tolerance for distributed data processing. By combining in-memory data grids, distributed SQL, real-time computation, and seamless integration with other big data tools, Apache Ignite provides a comprehensive platform for building high-performance, scalable applications. Its ability to distribute data across multiple nodes while providing low-latency access, fault tolerance, and high availability makes it an ideal choice for applications that require fast data access and complex processing.

Chapter 4: In-Memory Computing Fundamentals

In-memory computing refers to the practice of storing data in the main memory (RAM) rather than on traditional disk storage, enabling significantly faster access times and reduced latency for applications that need to process large amounts of data quickly. The concept of in-memory computing is foundational for modern high-performance systems, where data needs to be accessed and processed in real-time or near-real-time. This approach leverages the high-speed capabilities of RAM to speed up data processing, as traditional disk storage can create significant bottlenecks in systems requiring fast and frequent data access. In-memory computing has become a core component in various use cases, including real-time analytics, caching, machine learning, and distributed computing systems, allowing businesses to derive insights faster and improve application performance.

The key advantage of in-memory computing is the **reduction in data retrieval times**. Traditional disk-based storage, even with the fastest SSDs, can be orders of magnitude slower than accessing data stored in RAM. The read/write latency for memory is extremely low, typically in the range of nanoseconds, while disk access can take milliseconds, which is a significant difference when processing large datasets or responding to user interactions in real-time. This makes in-memory computing ideal for applications that require high throughput and low-latency access to data, such as high-frequency trading platforms, fraud detection systems, e-commerce sites, and social media networks.

In-memory computing relies on several core principles and technologies to enable fast data access and processing. One of the most fundamental aspects of in-memory computing is the **data grid** or **data store**. A data grid is a distributed system that stores data in the memory of a cluster of machines, allowing data to be accessed and processed by multiple nodes in parallel. This approach provides both **horizontal scalability** and **fault tolerance**, ensuring that the system can handle growing amounts of data and traffic without compromising performance. A **distributed data grid** allows large datasets to be split across multiple nodes in the system, where each node handles a portion of the data. This distribution ensures that data can be processed concurrently, taking advantage of the available memory and processing power across the entire system.

A common use case for in-memory computing is **caching**, where frequently accessed data is stored in memory to reduce the need for repetitive database queries or expensive computations. Caching works by storing the results of common database queries or the outputs of time-consuming calculations in memory so that future requests for the same data can be served from the cache, reducing the time and resources spent on data retrieval. This significantly improves performance in scenarios like web applications, where loading content from memory is far faster than querying a database. Popular caching solutions like **Memcached** and **Redis** provide in-memory stores for this purpose, enabling systems to serve data with minimal latency and high throughput.

Another crucial component of in-memory computing is the concept of **data partitioning**. Partitioning divides data into smaller, manageable chunks, known as partitions, which are distributed across multiple nodes in a cluster. This allows each node to handle a subset of the overall data, ensuring that data processing is parallelized and that workloads are balanced efficiently. When data is partitioned, each node can access its partition locally, minimizing the need for cross-node communication, which can add latency to the system. In-memory data grids often use **affinity** to ensure that related data is stored together on the same node, further optimizing performance by reducing the need for remote access.

To ensure **high availability** and **fault tolerance**, in-memory computing systems typically incorporate **data replication**. Data replication involves maintaining multiple copies of the same data across different nodes in the system. If one node fails, another node that holds a replica of the data can take over, ensuring that the system remains operational. This approach is particularly important in mission-critical applications where uptime is essential, and data loss or system downtime is not acceptable. Apache Ignite and **Hazelcast** are examples of in-memory computing platforms that support data replication, ensuring that data is available even if individual nodes fail.

Persistence is another key consideration in in-memory computing. While storing data in memory offers significant speed advantages, the data is typically lost when the system is restarted or when a node crashes. This creates a challenge for applications that need data durability. Some in-memory computing platforms, like Apache Ignite and **Redis**, provide persistence options, allowing data to be periodically written to disk or using **write-ahead logging** to ensure data is not lost in the event of a failure. These systems can be configured to balance the trade-off between in-memory performance and data durability based on the needs of the application. For example, if data loss is acceptable, the system may operate entirely in-memory without persistence, but for use cases where data durability is critical, periodic snapshots or append-only logging can be enabled to preserve data across restarts. Another fundamental principle of in-memory computing is **real-time data processing**. By storing data in memory, systems can process data as it arrives, allowing for real-time analytics, decision-making, and automated actions. This is particularly valuable in use cases such as fraud detection, where transactions need to be analyzed in real time, or predictive maintenance, where sensor data is continuously monitored to detect potential failures before they occur. In-memory computing allows systems to process and analyze data instantly, providing timely insights that can drive actions such as alerts, recommendations, or automatic adjustments.

Distributed computing frameworks also play a crucial role in in-memory computing, enabling complex computations to be executed across multiple nodes simultaneously. This allows for the processing of large datasets that cannot fit into the memory of a single machine. **Apache Spark**, for example, is an in-memory data processing engine that allows users to perform distributed data analysis and machine learning at scale. It stores intermediate data in memory, drastically reducing the time it takes to process data compared to traditional disk-based systems. Similarly, in-memory databases such as **SAP HANA** and **Oracle TimesTen** are optimized for high-speed transaction processing by keeping data in memory and allowing complex queries to be executed with minimal latency.

Concurrency control is another important aspect of in-memory computing. Because data is often accessed concurrently by multiple nodes or clients, mechanisms must be in place to ensure that concurrent operations do not lead to inconsistent or corrupted data. **Distributed locking** and **transactional systems** are used to manage concurrency and ensure that operations such as updates or inserts are completed in a way that maintains data consistency. Apache Ignite, for example, supports **ACID transactions**, allowing for transactional consistency across the cluster. These mechanisms ensure that despite the distributed nature of the system, the integrity of the data is maintained during concurrent access. Security is also a key consideration in in-memory computing systems. Data that is stored in memory needs to be protected from unauthorized access or tampering. Many in-memory computing platforms offer **encryption** for both data at rest and in transit, ensuring that sensitive information is kept secure. Additionally, role-based access control (RBAC) can be implemented to restrict access to specific data or operations within the system, allowing organizations to enforce strict security policies.

In-memory computing, with its high performance, low-latency access, and scalability, has become an essential component for modern applications that require real-time data processing, analytics, and decision-making. Whether used for caching, real-time analytics, or distributed computing, in-memory computing offers significant advantages over traditional disk-based systems, enabling businesses to process and derive insights from large amounts of data faster than ever before.

In Apache Ignite, **data grids** and **caching** are fundamental components that play a key role in enhancing the performance, scalability, and reliability of distributed systems. A **data grid** in Apache Ignite is a distributed, in-memory storage system that enables efficient storage and retrieval of data across multiple nodes. It allows data to be partitioned and distributed across a cluster of machines, enabling horizontal scalability and fault tolerance. By utilizing in-memory storage, a data grid provides fast access to large datasets, making it an essential tool for applications that require real-time processing and low-latency access to data. The **caching** feature in Apache Ignite works hand-in-hand with the data grid to store frequently accessed data in memory, reducing the need for time-consuming disk operations and enhancing system responsiveness.

One of the key benefits of using Apache Ignite's data grid is its **distributed nature**, which allows it to scale horizontally by adding more nodes to the cluster. As more nodes are added, the data is automatically partitioned and distributed across the available machines. Each node in the cluster holds a portion of the data, and Ignite's partitioning mechanism ensures that the data is evenly distributed, which helps achieve load balancing and improves overall system performance. This partitioning model is transparent to the user, meaning that the data grid can scale seamlessly without requiring manual intervention or complex configurations. The system handles data distribution automatically, ensuring that as the dataset grows, the grid can scale to meet the increased demand.

In Apache Ignite, data is organized into **caches**, which are the core units of storage within the data grid. A cache is a distributed, in-memory data structure that stores data in key-value pairs. Caches can be configured with different modes, such as **partitioned** or **replicated** caching, depending on the application's requirements. In **partitioned caching**, the cache data is divided into partitions, and each node is responsible for storing one or more partitions. This approach allows data to be distributed across the cluster, and each node holds only a portion of the total dataset. **Replicated caching**, on the other hand, maintains a copy of the cache on each node, ensuring that every node in the cluster has access to the entire dataset. This approach provides higher data redundancy and availability but may consume more memory as the same data is stored on every node.

When using **partitioned caches**, the number of partitions is a critical factor in achieving optimal performance and scalability. Apache Ignite uses a **hash-based partitioning strategy**, where data is divided into partitions based on a hashing function applied to the cache key. The number of partitions can be configured at the time of cache creation, and the system will automatically distribute the partitions across the nodes in the cluster. The **affinity** function in Ignite ensures that related data is placed on the same node or on nodes that are close to each other in the network, minimizing the need for cross-node communication and improving performance. The ability to partition data efficiently ensures that Ignite can handle large datasets with low-latency access, even as the system scales.

A significant advantage of using Apache Ignite as a data grid and cache is its **support for SQL queries**. Ignite provides an SQL engine that allows users to run SQL queries directly on the data stored in the grid. This SQL engine is fully integrated with the data grid, enabling users to perform complex queries such as JOINs, aggregations, and filtering on distributed data, all while taking advantage of the in-memory speed of the system. This capability allows users to interact with their data in a familiar way, using standard SQL syntax, without needing to write complex, low-level code to access the distributed data.

Another powerful feature of Apache Ignite's data grid is its **transactional support**. Ignite supports **ACID transactions**, meaning that it can handle operations that require **atomicity**, **consistency**, **isolation**, and **durability**. This ensures that data operations are consistent and reliable, even in a distributed environment. Ignite transactions can span across multiple nodes, and the system guarantees that the data remains consistent across the cluster, even in the event of failures. This makes Ignite an ideal choice for applications that require strong consistency, such as financial systems, e-commerce platforms, or inventory management systems, where data accuracy and reliability are critical.

Caching in Apache Ignite is another core feature that significantly enhances the performance of data-intensive applications. Caching is used to store frequently accessed data in memory so that it can be quickly retrieved without having to query the underlying database or perform expensive computations. Apache Ignite supports multiple **cache types**, including **local** caches, **distributed** caches, and **near** caches. The **local cache** stores data on a single node, providing fast access to data for that node. The **distributed cache** allows data to be shared across multiple nodes, ensuring that data is available to the entire cluster. The **near cache** is a local cache that stores a copy of data that is frequently accessed from the distributed cache, minimizing the need for remote calls and improving performance for repeated accesses.

A critical aspect of caching in Apache Ignite is **cache eviction**. As caches are stored in memory, there is a limited amount of space available. When the cache reaches its memory limit, data that is no longer needed must be evicted to make room for new data. Apache Ignite supports multiple **eviction strategies**, such as **Least Recently Used (LRU)**, **Least Frequently Used (LFU)**, and **random eviction**, allowing the system to evict the least valuable data first. These strategies can be configured based on the application's needs, helping ensure that the most important data remains in memory for fast access. Additionally, Apache Ignite supports **time-to-live (TTL)** settings for cache entries, allowing data to be automatically evicted after a specified time period, ensuring that stale or outdated data is removed from the cache.

Apache Ignite also provides **integration with big data platforms** like **Apache Hadoop** and **Apache Spark**, enabling users to take advantage of distributed computing frameworks to process large datasets stored in the Ignite data grid. Ignite can serve as an in-memory storage layer for Hadoop or Spark, allowing for faster data access and real-time processing of big data. This integration makes Apache Ignite an excellent choice for applications that require both high-performance data storage and powerful data processing capabilities.

One of the advantages of using Apache Ignite for caching is its **high availability**. Ignite provides built-in **data replication** and **fault tolerance**, ensuring that cached data is always available, even if some nodes in the cluster fail. Ignite can replicate data across multiple nodes, so if one node goes down, the data remains accessible from another node with a replica. This ensures that the system continues to operate smoothly, providing high availability for mission-critical applications that require 24/7 uptime.

Apache Ignite's **distributed data grid** and **caching** capabilities are essential for building high-performance, scalable applications that require fast, low-latency access to large datasets. By storing data in memory and distributing it across a cluster of nodes, Ignite can process data at lightning speed, making it ideal for use cases such as real-time analytics, distributed computing, and caching in high-traffic web applications. The ability to use SQL queries, support for transactions, and integration with big data platforms makes Apache Ignite a versatile tool for a wide range of applications that demand fast, reliable, and scalable data processing solutions.

Chapter 6: Scaling with Apache Ignite Clustering

Scaling with Apache Ignite clustering is a powerful approach to building high-performance, distributed data systems that can handle increasing workloads efficiently. Apache Ignite is designed to scale horizontally, meaning that as the demand for data processing and storage grows, new nodes can be added to the cluster without affecting the system's performance or availability. The clustering mechanism in Apache Ignite is built to support both **data partitioning** and **replication**, which enables the system to scale seamlessly, handle large datasets, and provide fault tolerance. This makes it a suitable solution for applications that require real-time data access, such as financial services, e-commerce platforms, and IoT systems, where high scalability and low latency are critical.

The first step in scaling with Apache Ignite is understanding the **cluster architecture**. An Ignite cluster consists of multiple nodes, each of which can act as a data node, a client node, or both. **Data nodes** store and process the distributed data, while **client nodes** interact with the cluster but do not store data. In a typical Ignite deployment, data nodes are responsible for maintaining the data grid and performing computations, while client nodes handle data access from the application. This separation allows for more efficient use of resources, as client nodes do not need to store large amounts of data, making them lighter and more focused on serving user requests.

Apache Ignite uses a **partitioned data model** for distributing data across the cluster. In this model, data is divided into smaller **partitions**, which are then distributed across the nodes in the cluster. Each node in the cluster is responsible for a subset of the partitions, and the data is automatically balanced as nodes are added or removed from the cluster. This partitioning strategy enables horizontal scaling, as new nodes can be added to increase the available memory and processing power of the cluster. When a new node joins the cluster, the system automatically redistributes the data partitions to ensure an even distribution across the available nodes. This allows the system to scale seamlessly without requiring manual intervention.

Each partition in the data grid is stored in memory across the nodes, allowing for **low-latency access** to the data. Because Apache Ignite is an in-memory data grid, all data is stored in **RAM**, which significantly reduces the time required to access and process the data compared to traditional disk-based systems. The in-memory architecture of Ignite allows for sub-millisecond response times, making it suitable for use cases that require real-time analytics, transactional processing, and other high-performance applications.

To ensure data availability and fault tolerance, Apache Ignite supports **data replication**. In a replicated cache, data is duplicated across multiple nodes in the cluster. This means that if one node fails, another node with a replica of the data can take over, ensuring that the system remains operational. Replication provides **high availability**, as data is not lost when a node crashes. Ignite's **replica count** setting determines how many copies of each partition should be maintained across the cluster. By default, Ignite maintains one replica per partition, but this can be adjusted to suit the application's needs. For instance, if your system requires more redundancy, you can increase the replica count to ensure that data is highly available even in the event of multiple node failures.

In addition to partitioning and replication, Ignite also supports **affinity**. Affinity ensures that related data is stored on the same node or on nodes that are close to each other in the network. This is especially important for performance, as it minimizes the need for cross-node communication during data access. When data is collocated or **affinely mapped**, queries and computations that involve related data can be executed on a single node, reducing the latency caused by moving data between nodes. Affinity configurations are vital for applications that require optimized performance, such as large-scale data processing, real-time analytics, and event-driven systems.

Load balancing is another important feature of Apache Ignite's clustering architecture. As new nodes are added to the cluster, Ignite automatically balances the data across the nodes to ensure that no single node becomes overloaded. This dynamic load balancing allows the cluster to handle increased traffic and workloads without performance degradation. The system continuously monitors the state of the cluster and adjusts the distribution of partitions to ensure that the cluster remains balanced. By using **auto-discovery** and **dynamic data rebalancing**, Ignite simplifies the scaling process, allowing you to add or remove nodes without affecting the operation of the cluster.

For **data consistency**, Apache Ignite uses **distributed ACID transactions**. When scaling a system across multiple nodes, maintaining consistency can become a challenge. Ignite addresses this by providing support for **distributed transactions**, ensuring that operations across different nodes are atomic, consistent, isolated, and durable. This makes it possible to maintain data integrity even as the cluster grows and data is distributed across multiple machines. Distributed transactions are essential in applications that require strong consistency, such as banking systems, supply chain management, and online order processing systems.

In addition to its robust data management capabilities, Apache Ignite also offers **compute grid** functionality, which allows for distributed computation across the cluster. Ignite's compute grid allows users to execute tasks in parallel on multiple nodes, enabling **high-performance distributed computing**. Tasks such as **map-reduce** operations, **machine learning** algorithms, and **graph processing** can be distributed across the cluster, taking advantage of the memory and processing power of each node. The compute grid in Apache Ignite is designed to scale with the size of the cluster, allowing for efficient parallelization of large-scale computations. This feature is crucial for big data analytics, real-time decision-making, and other use cases that require complex computations to be performed on large datasets in real time.

When scaling with Apache Ignite clustering, **security** is also an important consideration. Apache Ignite provides robust security features to ensure that the distributed data grid is protected against unauthorized access. Ignite supports **role-based access control (RBAC)**, which allows administrators to define user roles and permissions for accessing and modifying data. Encryption is also supported, both for data at rest and in transit, ensuring that sensitive information is protected. Security features are critical when deploying Apache Ignite in environments where data privacy and compliance with regulations are essential, such as in healthcare, finance, and government systems.

To manage and monitor a growing Ignite cluster, **monitoring tools** and **management consoles** are essential. Apache Ignite provides integration with **Apache Zookeeper** and third-party monitoring tools such as **Prometheus**, **Grafana**, and **Datadog** to provide insights into the health, performance, and resource utilization of the cluster. These tools allow administrators to track key metrics such as memory usage, cache hit/miss ratios, query performance, and system load, helping to identify and address potential issues before they affect the application's performance.

Scaling with Apache Ignite clustering allows you to build a high-performance, distributed system that can handle large amounts of data and traffic, all while maintaining low-latency access and high availability. The ability to partition data, replicate it across multiple nodes, and perform distributed computations makes Apache Ignite a powerful tool for building scalable, fault-tolerant data systems. Whether you're using Ignite for real-time analytics, data caching, or complex distributed computing tasks, its architecture provides the scalability and performance needed to meet the demands of modern applications.

Chapter 7: Advanced Data Storage and Persistence in Ignite

Apache Ignite is a powerful distributed in-memory computing platform that provides advanced features for **data storage** and **persistence**. While its primary strength lies in **in-memory computing**, which ensures fast access and high throughput for data-intensive applications, Ignite also offers robust persistence mechanisms that allow applications to store data durably and reliably. Apache Ignite is uniquely suited to modern applications that demand real-time data processing, scalability, and high availability, while also requiring the ability to retain data across system restarts, node failures, or scaling events. Understanding the advanced data storage and persistence features of Ignite is essential for utilizing its full potential in scenarios that require both speed and durability. At its core, **Apache Ignite's data storage** relies heavily on in-memory storage to provide sub-millisecond latency for both reads and writes. The system stores data in **RAM** rather than on traditional disk storage, which significantly reduces the time required to access and process the data compared to disk-based systems. This in-memory approach provides a performance advantage by allowing for fast data retrieval without being hindered by the slower access speeds associated with disk I/O. However, for applications that require data durability and the ability to recover data after system restarts or crashes, Apache Ignite also offers **persistence mechanisms** that seamlessly integrate with its in-memory architecture.

One of the most important concepts in Ignite's architecture is its **data grid**, where data is partitioned and distributed across a cluster of nodes. In this **distributed data grid**, data is split into smaller units called **partitions**, and each partition is assigned to one or more nodes. Apache Ignite uses a **partitioned** model for data storage, where each node stores a subset of the data, ensuring that the system can scale horizontally by adding more nodes as needed. This **horizontal scaling** ensures that data storage and processing capacity can grow dynamically to meet the needs of modern applications. In addition to partitioning, **data replication** ensures that copies of data are stored across multiple nodes for redundancy, improving data availability and fault tolerance. Ignite's persistence capabilities allow for **durable storage** while maintaining high performance. While it is designed to keep most data in memory, Apache Ignite can store data on disk through its **persistence layer**, ensuring that data is not lost in the event of a failure. Ignite provides two key options for persistence: **RDB (Redis Database) snapshots** and **AOF (Append-Only File)** logging, similar to what is available in Redis. RDB snapshots provide a way to periodically save the entire dataset to disk, while AOF logging records every change made to the data in the form of log entries. This allows Ignite to rebuild its in-memory data grid after a failure by reloading data from disk, ensuring that no data is lost between restarts.

RDB snapshots are a way to persist data by taking periodic snapshots of the data at specific intervals. These snapshots are stored on disk and can be used to restore the system to its last known state in the event of a failure. Ignite allows users to configure the frequency of RDB snapshots through the snapshotInterval parameter, which controls how often the snapshots are taken. The benefit of RDB snapshots is that they provide fast recovery times because they store the entire dataset in a compact binary format. However, there is a trade-off between performance and durability since taking snapshots too frequently can negatively affect performance due to the time spent writing data to disk.

On the other hand, **AOF (Append-Only File)** logging provides a more granular and durable approach to persistence. AOF logs every write operation performed on the data, ensuring that every change is captured and stored on disk. This means that if the system crashes, Ignite can replay the AOF logs to rebuild the data grid and ensure that no changes are lost. AOF logging is useful for applications that require **strong durability** and cannot afford to lose any data. A key advantage of AOF over RDB snapshots is that it provides **point-in-time recovery** since every write operation is recorded in the log. However, AOF logging can add additional overhead to write-heavy applications, as each write operation must be logged to disk before it is acknowledged.

Hybrid Persistence is another advanced feature in Apache Ignite, allowing for the use of both RDB snapshots and AOF logging together. This hybrid approach provides a balance between performance and durability by allowing Ignite to take periodic snapshots while also logging write operations to disk. By combining these two mechanisms, Ignite can offer both fast recovery times and strong durability. This approach can be configured by setting both snapshotInterval for RDB snapshots and aofEnabled for AOF logging. The hybrid persistence model is ideal for applications that need to ensure high availability and data integrity while maintaining high-speed in-memory performance.

Apache Ignite also supports **near cache** functionality, which is particularly useful for reducing latency in distributed applications. A **near cache** is a local cache on each node that stores a subset of the data from the distributed cache, providing faster access to frequently requested data. This helps reduce the number of remote calls to other nodes in the cluster, which can add significant latency. The near cache is especially valuable in applications where some data is highly localized and frequently accessed by individual nodes, while other data can be kept in the distributed cache for broader use. The near cache ensures that these frequently accessed data items are readily available in memory on the local node, further improving the responsiveness of the system.

In terms of **data consistency**, Apache Ignite supports **ACID (Atomicity, Consistency, Isolation, Durability) transactions** for its in-memory data grid. These transactions allow Ignite to manage data operations in a way that ensures **consistency** across the cluster. This means that all updates to the data are fully isolated from each other, ensuring that they do not interfere with one another and remain consistent, even in the event of failures. Ignite uses **two-phase commit (2PC)** to coordinate transactions across multiple nodes, ensuring that all nodes involved in a transaction either commit the changes or roll them back if any issues arise. This provides strong consistency guarantees, which is important for applications that require accurate and reliable data processing, such as financial systems and e-commerce platforms.

To enhance the performance of data storage, Apache Ignite also supports **off-heap memory** storage. By storing data in **off-heap memory**, Ignite can store data outside the Java heap, reducing the burden on garbage collection and ensuring that large datasets can be managed efficiently. Off-heap memory allows Ignite to store large amounts of data without running into memory management issues that can occur when relying solely on Java heap space. This is particularly important in large-scale, memory-intensive applications where avoiding frequent garbage collection pauses is crucial for maintaining high performance.

In addition to data grid and caching, Ignite's persistence system supports **disk-based indexing**. Ignite allows indexes to be created on persisted data, which enables fast querying and retrieval of stored data. These indexes improve the efficiency of SQL queries by reducing the need to scan the entire dataset. By creating indexes on frequently queried fields, Apache Ignite can significantly reduce the time it takes to retrieve data, providing faster response times for applications that need to execute complex queries on large datasets.

Apache Ignite provides advanced features for **data storage** and **persistence**, making it suitable for applications that require both in-memory performance and durability. Whether using RDB snapshots, AOF logging, or hybrid persistence, Ignite ensures that data is reliably stored and quickly retrievable, even in the face of failures. By combining in-memory storage with powerful persistence options and ensuring high availability and fault tolerance through replication and partitioning, Apache Ignite offers a comprehensive solution for modern, data-intensive applications. The flexibility in configuring persistence options, along with the ability to store and process data both in memory and on disk, allows users to build highly scalable and resilient systems.

Chapter 8: Ignite SQL and Querying for Real-Time Data

Apache Ignite provides powerful tools for real-time data querying and analytics through its integrated **SQL engine**. The combination of in-memory data processing with SQL-based querying allows applications to interact with large datasets efficiently and at high speed. Ignite SQL allows users to execute distributed queries over data stored in the cluster, taking advantage of Ignite's in-memory storage to deliver low-latency responses. By integrating standard SQL syntax with distributed computing, Apache Ignite provides an intuitive way to interact with data while ensuring high performance, making it ideal for real-time data processing and analytics in a variety of use cases such as e-commerce platforms, financial systems, and IoT applications.

At its core, **Ignite SQL** extends traditional relational database functionality by enabling distributed SQL processing across a cluster of nodes. This distributed model ensures that queries are processed in parallel, taking full advantage of the computing resources available within the cluster. Ignite's SQL engine works directly with the **in-memory data grid**, enabling fast access to data without relying on slower disk-based storage. This means that even large-scale datasets, which would traditionally take a long time to query, can be processed efficiently with Ignite's distributed approach to SQL queries. Additionally, Ignite supports **SQL joins**, **aggregations**, and **filtering**, making it suitable for complex data analysis and reporting.

Apache Ignite's SQL engine is fully integrated with its **distributed data grid**, meaning that all data stored in Ignite caches can be queried using SQL syntax. This includes **key-value stores, tables**, and **indexes** that are part of the Ignite data model. Ignite supports standard **ANSI SQL** syntax, so users familiar with relational databases can start using the SQL engine with minimal learning curve. Ignite SQL queries can be executed on large-scale distributed data structures with all the benefits of in-memory processing, significantly reducing query execution times.

One of the most important features of Ignite SQL is its ability to handle **distributed joins**. While relational databases typically perform joins within a single system, Ignite distributes the data across multiple nodes, which means that joins can span multiple nodes in the cluster. To support efficient querying, Ignite uses a **collocated join model**, where related data is stored on the same node, ensuring that joins between related datasets are performed locally, reducing network overhead. This model significantly improves performance by eliminating the need for remote data transfers when executing joins, ensuring that large datasets can be joined quickly and efficiently.

In addition to standard SQL functionality, Ignite SQL supports **indexed queries** to accelerate query execution. Ignite allows users to create indexes on specific fields of their data, which can greatly reduce query response times by providing a faster way to locate and retrieve the requested data. For example, if an application frequently queries a specific field such as customer ID or product category, indexes can be created on those fields to ensure that queries involving those attributes are processed more quickly. Ignite supports various types of indexes, including **hash indexes**, **B-tree indexes**, and **full-text indexes**, making it flexible for a wide range of querying needs.

Another key feature of Ignite SQL is its support for **transactions**. Ignite SQL queries can be executed within the context of **ACID-compliant transactions**, ensuring that the data remains consistent, even when multiple operations are performed concurrently across the cluster. This is particularly important in applications where data integrity is critical, such as financial systems, where transactions must be processed reliably across distributed nodes. By using distributed transactions in Ignite, users can ensure that changes to the data are consistent across the entire cluster, without worrying about partial or inconsistent updates.

For **real-time analytics**, Ignite SQL provides features like **windowed queries** and **streaming analytics**. Windowed queries allow users to perform continuous analysis on data streams as new data arrives, providing the ability to calculate metrics and derive insights in real-time. This is highly useful in applications that require near-instant analysis of data, such as monitoring financial markets, detecting fraud in e-commerce, or tracking sensor data from IoT devices. By combining SQL-based querying with real-time data processing capabilities, Apache Ignite enables complex analytics to be performed on live data with minimal delay.

Another aspect of Ignite's SQL querying capabilities is its **support for heterogeneous data sources**. Apache Ignite supports **SQL over both in-memory and persistent data**. This means that users can query data stored in Ignite's distributed caches as well as data stored on disk, such as relational databases, Hadoop, or NoSQL systems. This makes Ignite SQL a powerful tool for applications that need to aggregate or analyze data from multiple sources, allowing users to query all their data in a unified manner. Ignite also supports querying external systems via **JDBC** and **ODBC** drivers, enabling applications to access data from Ignite using standard database connectors.

The **SQL engine** in Apache Ignite also includes support for **joins across heterogeneous data sources**, meaning that users can join data stored in Ignite with data stored in external systems such as relational databases, Hadoop, or other big data platforms. This provides flexibility in real-time analytics, as users can query distributed data stored in different systems and join them together without needing to move the data between systems. This capability is essential for enterprises that rely on data from multiple sources, allowing them to perform real-time analytics and reporting without significant data movement or performance overhead.

One of the defining characteristics of Ignite SQL is **distributed query execution**, which allows queries to be executed in parallel across the cluster. When a query is submitted, Ignite's SQL engine breaks the query into smaller tasks, distributing these tasks across multiple nodes in the cluster. This enables the query to be processed faster and more efficiently, as each node works on a portion of the data simultaneously. Ignite also optimizes query execution by using **query execution plans**, which are created based on the structure of the data and the query. These execution plans allow Ignite to select the most efficient way to execute a query, taking into account factors such as data distribution, partitioning, and indexing.

One of the most significant advantages of using Ignite SQL for real-time data querying is **low-latency access**. Because Ignite is an in-memory computing platform, data is stored in RAM, which enables faster access times than traditional disk-based databases. In scenarios where real-time or near-real-time data processing is required, this low-latency access can make a significant difference in performance. By querying data in memory and utilizing parallel processing across the cluster, Ignite provides an excellent solution for applications that need fast, real-time results, such as fraud detection, recommendation engines, and monitoring systems.

Apache Ignite also integrates seamlessly with **Apache Kafka** for stream processing, allowing real-time data to be ingested and queried using SQL queries. This integration allows applications to process data as it arrives, perform real-time analytics, and execute SQL queries on the incoming data without delay. This is particularly useful for scenarios like monitoring financial transactions or analyzing log data in real-time, where rapid analysis of incoming streams is crucial.

The SQL capabilities of Apache Ignite extend beyond traditional relational database operations. By providing distributed, in-memory SQL querying, Ignite enables applications to execute complex analytics and perform fast, real-time data processing on large datasets. Whether working with in-memory caches, external data sources, or streaming data, Ignite SQL offers a comprehensive querying solution that allows organizations to harness the full power of their distributed data systems. The combination of high performance, flexibility, and real-time querying makes Apache Ignite an ideal choice for modern applications that require quick, reliable access to large datasets.

Chapter 9: Integrating Apache Ignite with Other Systems

Integrating Apache Ignite with other systems is a key aspect of utilizing its full potential for building high-performance, distributed data platforms. Apache Ignite can seamlessly integrate with various external systems to enhance its capabilities, improve performance, and provide flexible solutions for real-time analytics, data storage, and caching. One of the standout features of Apache Ignite is its ability to connect with various big data frameworks, databases, messaging systems, and cloud platforms, allowing organizations to create a unified ecosystem for managing large volumes of data. The integration process is made easier through the rich set of APIs, connectors, and protocols provided by Ignite, ensuring that it can be effectively used alongside other technologies in diverse environments.

A primary area where Apache Ignite is often integrated is in big data processing. Apache Ignite integrates **well with Apache Hadoop** and **Apache Spark**, two of the most widely used big data platforms. The integration with **Apache Hadoop** allows Ignite to act as a fast, in-memory storage layer for Hadoop's data processing workflows. Ignite's ability to store intermediate data in memory during MapReduce jobs significantly speeds up the overall processing time compared to relying on disk-based storage. This integration helps bridge the gap between the high-latency, disk-based data storage of Hadoop and the fast in-memory processing that Ignite provides, improving the performance of large-scale data processing tasks.

Apache Spark, another powerful big data framework, benefits greatly from Apache Ignite's in-memory capabilities. Spark is known for its ability to process large datasets in parallel, and by integrating with Ignite, Spark can take advantage of Ignite's distributed in-memory data grid. Ignite can serve as an in-memory cache for Spark's Resilient Distributed Datasets (RDDs), allowing faster data retrieval and reducing the time spent reading and writing data to disk. This integration ensures that the data required for Spark computations is readily available in memory, thus speeding up the execution of Spark jobs. Additionally, Apache Ignite provides the **IgniteRDD** API, which allows users to create and manage RDDs in Ignite, further streamlining the integration process and enabling real-time data analytics with minimal latency.

For **data persistence**, Apache Ignite can also be integrated with traditional relational databases and **NoSQL systems**. One of the primary advantages of using Ignite with relational databases is its ability to function as a distributed cache, reducing the load on the backend database and speeding up data retrieval. Apache Ignite supports integration with popular relational databases through **JDBC** and **ODBC** connectors. By caching frequently accessed data in Ignite's in-memory data grid, applications can reduce the number of expensive database queries, resulting in faster response times and reduced database load. This integration is useful in scenarios where applications require low-latency access to data, such as e-commerce platforms, financial systems, and real-time analytics.

When working with **NoSQL databases**, Apache Ignite complements technologies like **MongoDB, Cassandra**, and **HBase** by acting as an in-memory layer that accelerates data access and query execution. For example, Ignite can be used alongside **Cassandra** to improve query performance by caching frequently queried data from Cassandra's disk-based storage. Since Cassandra is optimized for write-heavy workloads, integrating it with Ignite allows the system to serve read requests from the in-memory cache, reducing the need to access disk storage and ensuring fast response times. Similarly, integrating Ignite with **MongoDB** provides low-latency access to data, which is crucial for applications like content delivery networks (CDNs), where real-time access to data is critical.

For **real-time messaging** and event-driven architectures, Apache Ignite can integrate with **Apache Kafka** and **RabbitMQ** to enable fast data streaming and message processing. Kafka, a distributed event streaming platform, can work with Ignite to provide a high-throughput, low-latency messaging system. When combined with Ignite, Kafka can stream real-time data to Ignite's in-memory data grid, where it can be processed and analyzed quickly. This is particularly valuable in use cases such as fraud detection in financial services, real-time inventory management, and IoT applications, where immediate processing of incoming events is crucial. Kafka's ability to handle massive streams of data combined with Ignite's in-memory processing enables fast and efficient data handling.

Another key integration is with **cloud platforms** such as **Amazon Web Services (AWS)**, **Microsoft Azure**, and **Google Cloud Platform (GCP)**. Apache Ignite can be deployed in the cloud to provide a scalable and distributed in-memory computing environment. With cloud-based deployment, organizations can easily scale their Ignite cluster by adding new virtual machines or instances to meet the growing demands of their applications. In addition to scaling, cloud platforms offer a range of services that can be leveraged in conjunction with Ignite, such as object storage, machine learning models, and data lakes. Apache Ignite can integrate with cloud storage systems like **Amazon S3** or **Azure Blob Storage** for data persistence, providing users with the flexibility to store large datasets while taking advantage of Ignite's in-memory processing capabilities. Apache Ignite also supports integration with **machine learning frameworks**, enabling real-time analytics and decision-making. By combining Ignite's in-memory data grid with machine learning frameworks like **Apache Spark MLlib** or **TensorFlow**, organizations can process and analyze data in real time to build intelligent applications. Ignite's ability to store and process large datasets in memory makes it an ideal solution for real-time machine learning applications, where the need for low-latency data access and rapid model training is crucial. Ignite's **Compute Grid** can distribute machine learning tasks across the cluster, accelerating the training and inference processes, while ensuring that the model data is readily available in memory for fast predictions.

For **streaming data** applications, Apache Ignite integrates with **Apache Flink** and **Apache Storm**, providing support for real-time stream processing and analytics. Apache Flink, known for its ability to process large streams of data in real-time, can be integrated with Ignite to store intermediate results in memory, providing fast access to streaming data. Ignite's **continuous query** feature allows real-time updates and processing of data as it enters the system, ensuring that applications can react instantly to changes in the incoming data stream. This is particularly useful for applications in industries such as telecommunications, media, and healthcare, where streaming data needs to be processed with minimal delay.

To integrate Apache Ignite with other systems, Ignite provides a variety of connectors, APIs, and integration points. These include **JDBC/ODBC drivers**, which enable Ignite to communicate with relational databases, **Ignite Machine Learning APIs**, **SQL-based connectors**, and native integrations with big data systems. With these tools, organizations can leverage Ignite's fast in-memory storage and processing alongside other technologies in their existing data ecosystem, enabling them to build powerful, scalable, and low-latency data platforms.

By integrating Apache Ignite with external systems, businesses can enhance their data architectures, improve application performance, and meet the demands of real-time processing. Whether using Ignite as a distributed cache, a high-performance data grid, or a machine learning processing engine, its ability to integrate with a wide variety of systems makes it a versatile tool for modern data-driven applications.

Chapter 10: Performance Tuning and Optimization in Apache Ignite

Performance tuning and optimization in Apache Ignite are essential steps for ensuring that your in-memory data grid operates at its full potential. Apache Ignite is a distributed, in-memory computing platform, and like any large-scale, distributed system, it requires careful configuration and tuning to ensure that it handles data efficiently, scales smoothly, and delivers high performance under varying workloads. Apache Ignite's ability to process massive amounts of data in memory is one of its primary strengths, but to get the most out of the platform, it's crucial to understand and optimize various aspects of its configuration, such as **memory management, data partitioning, caching, query performance, network settings**, and **transaction handling**.

One of the key factors in tuning Apache Ignite's performance is **memory management**. Since Apache Ignite is an in-memory data grid, the amount of available memory is directly tied to the system's overall performance. To optimize performance, it is important to carefully configure the amount of memory allocated to Ignite's **data structures** and **caches**. Apache Ignite allows for **off-heap memory**, which enables data to be stored outside the Java heap to avoid the performance overhead of garbage collection. By storing data off-heap, Ignite can handle large datasets without the risk of memory fragmentation or GC pauses that can degrade performance. Tuning the **off-heap memory** settings is critical for ensuring that large amounts of data can be stored and accessed without introducing latency caused by garbage collection cycles. For systems with high memory demands, off-heap memory provides the flexibility to store large datasets and process them quickly without running into memory management limitations.

Another key area for optimizing memory usage is **cache configuration**. Apache Ignite provides **caching** to store frequently accessed data in memory, allowing it to be quickly retrieved without having to access slower data sources like databases or disks. Ignite supports both **partitioned** and **replicated caches**, each offering its advantages and performance characteristics. In **partitioned caching**, the cache data is split into partitions, and each node in the cluster is responsible for a subset of the data. This helps distribute the data evenly across the cluster and enables horizontal scalability. **Replicated caches**, on the other hand, store copies of the data on each node, which ensures high availability but may lead to increased memory usage. By carefully choosing the appropriate cache strategy based on the specific requirements of the application, such as read and write patterns, the system can optimize memory usage and improve cache performance. Additionally, cache eviction policies, such as **Least Recently Used (LRU)** or **Least Frequently Used (LFU)**, should be configured based on the data access patterns to ensure that the most relevant data remains in memory and that older, less relevant data is evicted.

Data partitioning is another critical aspect of performance tuning in Apache Ignite. Data in an Ignite cluster is partitioned and distributed across multiple nodes, which allows the system to scale horizontally. To optimize performance, the number of **partitions** should be carefully configured based on the size of the dataset and the number of nodes in the cluster. Having too many partitions can result in excessive overhead for managing the partitions, while too few partitions can lead to unbalanced data distribution and hotspots in the system. Apache Ignite provides the ability to configure the number of partitions using the partitionCount setting, and choosing an optimal number of partitions helps balance the data distribution and ensures that the system scales efficiently. Furthermore, **affinity** is an important concept when tuning data partitioning. Affinity ensures that related data is placed together on the same node, which reduces the need for cross-node communication when performing queries or computations. By fine-tuning the affinity settings, Ignite can optimize data locality, improve query performance, and reduce network overhead.

Query performance is another area that requires careful tuning to ensure that Ignite delivers fast results for complex queries. Ignite supports **SQL queries** and provides an SQL engine that allows users to run distributed queries across the data grid. For high-performance query processing, **indexes** are essential. Creating appropriate indexes on frequently queried fields can significantly improve query execution times by reducing the amount of data that needs to be scanned during query processing. Apache Ignite supports several types of indexes, including **hash indexes**, **B-tree indexes**, and **full-text indexes**, which can be used based on the specific query patterns and data access requirements. For example, indexing fields that are frequently used in **JOINs**, **WHERE clauses**, or **ORDER BY** clauses can help optimize query performance. It's also important to configure **SQL queries** to avoid full-table scans, which can slow down query processing. By properly configuring indexes and query execution plans, you can optimize the performance of SQL queries running on large datasets.

Another important area for optimization is **network configuration**. Apache Ignite is a distributed system, and the communication between nodes in the cluster plays a crucial role in performance. To minimize network overhead, it's important to configure **network settings** and **communication protocols** properly. Apache Ignite uses **TCP** for node discovery and communication, and optimizing the network topology can improve the system's overall performance. For example, reducing the number of **network hops** or optimizing the network interface settings can decrease latency and improve throughput. Additionally, the configuration of the **communication SPI (Service Provider Interface)** can affect how efficiently data is transferred between nodes. Ensuring that the network is properly configured to handle high traffic volumes and large data transfers can reduce bottlenecks and improve overall system responsiveness.

Transaction handling is another critical aspect of performance tuning in Apache Ignite. While Ignite supports **ACID transactions**, which ensure data consistency and reliability, transaction processing can introduce overhead if not managed properly. To optimize transaction performance, it is important to configure the **transaction timeout**, **isolation level**, and **commit policy** according to the requirements of the application. In high-throughput systems, reducing the transaction scope and duration can help minimize the impact of transactions on performance. Apache Ignite supports **optimistic and pessimistic** transaction modes, and choosing the appropriate transaction mode based on the application's needs can help improve performance. Additionally, **transaction replication** settings should be tuned to ensure that transactions are efficiently replicated across nodes in the cluster while maintaining high availability. Finally, **cluster management** is essential for optimizing performance at scale. Apache Ignite provides **cluster auto-discovery** and **dynamic data rebalancing** to ensure that the system remains balanced as new nodes are added or removed from the cluster. By enabling auto-discovery, new nodes can be automatically integrated into the cluster without manual intervention, and the system will automatically rebalance data to ensure that it is distributed evenly across the available nodes. This ensures that the system can scale efficiently as the application grows, maintaining optimal performance even under increasing loads. Additionally, Apache Ignite provides **monitoring tools** to track the health and performance of the cluster, including **metrics for memory usage**, **cache hit/miss ratios**, **query performance**, and **network latency**. These tools allow administrators to monitor the system and make adjustments as needed to ensure that the system continues to perform optimally.

Tuning and optimizing Apache Ignite for performance involves configuring various components of the system, such as memory management, data partitioning, caching, query performance, network settings, and transaction handling. By understanding and optimizing these areas, you can ensure that your Ignite deployment can handle increasing workloads, maintain low-latency access to data, and scale seamlessly to meet the demands of modern, data-intensive applications. Each tuning decision should be made based on the specific use case and workload, allowing Apache Ignite to deliver its full potential in high-performance, distributed computing environments.

Chapter 11: Building Fault-Tolerant and High-Availability Systems

Building fault-tolerant and high-availability systems is a critical aspect of modern software architecture, particularly for applications that require constant uptime and robust performance. The goal of a fault-tolerant system is to continue functioning even in the presence of failures, whether they are hardware malfunctions, software bugs, or network disruptions. High-availability (HA) systems go hand in hand with fault tolerance, ensuring that services remain accessible even during failures or periods of high demand. To achieve these goals, multiple strategies must be employed, including **data replication**, **load balancing**, **failover mechanisms**, **distributed architectures**, and **resilient communication protocols**. By combining these strategies, developers can design systems that are resilient to both expected and unexpected failures, ensuring that applications deliver continuous and reliable services.

One of the most fundamental principles of fault-tolerant systems is **data replication**, where copies of data are stored on multiple nodes across a system. This ensures that if one node fails, the data is still available from another replica, preventing downtime and data loss. **Distributed databases** and **in-memory data grids** like Apache Ignite, **Cassandra**, and **MongoDB** often use replication to maintain high availability. For example, in a replicated data setup, each piece of data has one or more copies, or **replicas**, which are distributed across different nodes in the system. These replicas can be kept in sync through various consistency models, such as **eventual consistency** or **strong consistency**, depending on the use case. By replicating data, the system can handle node failures and continue providing data to users with minimal impact. In systems like Apache Ignite, **partitioned** caching and **data grids** ensure that data is both stored in memory and replicated across multiple nodes, allowing the system to recover quickly after failures.

To further enhance fault tolerance, **automatic failover** mechanisms are employed. These mechanisms ensure that when a failure is detected, the system can automatically switch to a backup resource, node, or replica, without requiring manual intervention. Failover processes can be automatic or semi-automatic, depending on how quickly the system can detect failures and how much human oversight is necessary. For example, in distributed systems, a **load balancer** may detect when a node fails and automatically reroute traffic to healthy nodes. In the case of a cloud environment, platforms like **Amazon Web Services (AWS)** or **Microsoft Azure** offer tools that automatically spin up replacement instances when a node fails, allowing for seamless failover in the cloud infrastructure. These tools can be configured to check the health of services and trigger automatic actions based on pre-configured thresholds or patterns of failure, ensuring minimal disruption to users and business operations.

Load balancing is a critical technique in fault-tolerant system design. By distributing incoming traffic or requests evenly across multiple servers or nodes, load balancing ensures that no single node is overwhelmed, preventing system crashes due to high load and making the system more resilient. In the case of high-traffic applications, such as web servers or APIs, load balancing plays a crucial role in managing traffic spikes. Load balancers can be configured to detect unhealthy nodes and route traffic away from them to healthy instances, which not only ensures continuous service during failures but also enhances overall performance. Common techniques used for load balancing include **round-robin**, **least connections**, and **IP hash** methods. For dynamic scaling, cloud platforms like AWS or GCP can automatically adjust load balancing based on real-time traffic patterns, further enhancing the fault tolerance of the system.

In distributed systems, **data partitioning** is another key element for building fault-tolerant and high-availability systems. Data partitioning divides large datasets into smaller, more manageable pieces, or **partitions**, which are distributed across multiple nodes. Each partition contains a subset of the data, and if one partition's node fails, another replica or backup partition can take over, ensuring that data remains accessible. Apache Ignite, for instance, employs a partitioned data model where the data grid is split into multiple partitions, and each partition is managed by a separate node. As new nodes are added to the system, the data is automatically rebalanced across the cluster, ensuring that the load is distributed evenly. Partitioning allows the system to scale out horizontally, improving both fault tolerance and performance as the number of nodes increases.

In addition to data replication, **distributed transaction management** plays a vital role in ensuring the consistency and durability of the system. Distributed transactions ensure that operations spanning multiple nodes or partitions are handled atomically, meaning that either all parts of the transaction are committed successfully, or none of them are. This prevents partial updates that could lead to inconsistent data in the event of a failure. Many distributed systems, including Apache Ignite, provide support for **ACID (Atomicity, Consistency, Isolation, Durability)** transactions, ensuring that even in the case of a system crash, the integrity of the data is preserved. Systems such as **Apache Kafka** or **Apache Pulsar** use transactional guarantees for stream processing, ensuring that messages or events are processed reliably and in the correct order, even under failure scenarios.

Another key strategy for ensuring high availability and fault tolerance is **geographic redundancy**. Geographic redundancy involves deploying application components across multiple physical or virtual locations, such as different data centers or availability zones. This is particularly important for global applications where downtime in one region could have far-reaching consequences. By replicating data and services across regions, organizations can ensure that even if an entire data center or availability zone becomes unavailable due to network outages, power failures, or natural disasters, the system continues to operate with minimal disruption. Cloud platforms like AWS, Google Cloud, and Microsoft Azure support multi-region deployment, enabling businesses to architect geographically redundant systems.

Monitoring and alerting also play a critical role in fault-tolerant system design. A robust monitoring system provides real-time visibility into the health of the system and helps detect failures before they impact users. Tools like **Prometheus**, **Grafana**, and **Datadog** can be integrated with distributed systems to monitor key metrics such as CPU usage, memory consumption, request latency, and error rates. These tools enable proactive management of the system, alerting administrators when thresholds are breached or when failures occur. By continuously monitoring system health, administrators can take preventive measures to resolve issues before they cause significant downtime.

Furthermore, **self-healing mechanisms** can be employed in fault-tolerant systems to automatically recover from failures. In modern distributed systems, technologies like **Kubernetes** provide **auto-healing** capabilities, where containers or services are automatically restarted when they fail. Kubernetes, in combination with **Docker** or other containerization technologies, makes it easier to manage distributed applications by allowing them to be rescheduled on healthy nodes or clusters. These auto-healing systems ensure that the infrastructure remains resilient, minimizing the impact of failures.

Service-oriented architectures (SOA) and **microservices** also contribute to fault tolerance and high availability. By breaking applications into smaller, independent services, fault isolation is achieved. If one service fails, it doesn't necessarily bring down the entire application. Microservices, along with service discovery tools like **Consul** or **Eureka**, allow systems to handle failures gracefully by ensuring that failed services are quickly detected and replaced with healthy instances, all while maintaining service continuity across the system.

In conclusion, building fault-tolerant and high-availability systems requires a multi-layered approach that combines **data replication, load balancing, failover mechanisms, distributed transaction management, geographic redundancy,** and **monitoring and alerting.** By implementing these strategies, businesses can create resilient systems that continue to provide uninterrupted service, even in the face of failures or high demand. Whether through the use of distributed caches, microservices, or cloud-based solutions, the goal is to design systems that are capable of recovering from failures quickly and efficiently, providing a seamless experience to users while ensuring business continuity.

Chapter 12: Real-World Use Cases: Apache Ignite in Action

Apache Ignite, as a high-performance, distributed in-memory computing platform, offers a wide range of real-world use cases that demonstrate its versatility and capability to handle complex, data-intensive tasks in real-time. Ignite's in-memory data grid, SQL querying, and distributed computing features make it suitable for industries and applications requiring high throughput, low-latency data processing, and scalability. One of the primary use cases of Apache Ignite is in **real-time analytics**, where companies need to process vast amounts of data quickly to derive insights and make decisions instantly. Apache Ignite's in-memory storage enables real-time analytics on massive datasets, allowing users to perform complex queries and aggregations with sub-millisecond latency. For example, in the **financial services industry**, trading platforms and stock exchanges rely on Ignite to process real-time market data and execute trades based on current conditions. The ability to store and query high-frequency financial data in memory ensures that transactions are processed with minimal delay, making it ideal for high-frequency trading systems.

Another key use case for Apache Ignite is **distributed caching**. Many applications, especially web applications, experience performance bottlenecks when they need to frequently retrieve data from backend databases. This is particularly true for **e-commerce websites**, where users may repeatedly query product listings, inventory data, and customer information. Apache Ignite can be used as a distributed cache layer in front of the database, storing frequently accessed data in memory. This reduces the load on the underlying database and accelerates response times by serving the data directly from the cache. With Ignite's ability to distribute data across multiple nodes, it ensures that the cache scales horizontally as the number of users and queries increases. This makes Apache Ignite a perfect solution for applications requiring high scalability and low-latency data retrieval, such as online shopping platforms that experience high traffic during peak seasons like Black Friday or Cyber Monday.

In **customer-facing applications** that require **real-time personalization**, Apache Ignite can be used to store user session data and preferences in memory, enabling faster access to personalized content or recommendations. For instance, a **streaming service** like Netflix or Spotify might use Apache Ignite to store user viewing or listening history and preferences, which can be quickly accessed to deliver personalized recommendations and advertisements. By storing this session data in memory and using Ignite's SQL engine to query the data in real-time, the platform can instantly provide customized experiences for each user. This is especially critical when dealing with millions of active users who require immediate, personalized recommendations based on their preferences, ensuring high-quality user engagement.

Internet of Things (IoT) is another domain where Apache Ignite is widely used. IoT systems generate massive amounts of sensor data that need to be processed in real-time to provide meaningful insights. Apache Ignite's in-memory processing capabilities make it well-suited for **real-time analytics** of IoT data. For example, in **smart cities**, sensors monitoring traffic, air quality, and energy consumption generate large volumes of data that need to be processed instantly. Apache Ignite can be deployed to store and process this sensor data in memory, allowing for real-time analysis, anomaly detection, and decision-making. Ignite's ability to integrate with other big data platforms such as **Apache Kafka** or **Apache Spark** ensures that streaming data can be ingested, processed, and analyzed in real-time, enabling **predictive maintenance**, **traffic management**, and **energy optimization**.

Apache Ignite also plays a significant role in **machine learning** and **data science applications**. The platform provides in-memory storage and distributed computing capabilities that are essential for processing large datasets and training machine learning models at scale. For example, in **retail**, companies may use Apache Ignite to store large customer transaction datasets, which can then be queried and analyzed using machine learning algorithms to derive insights into customer behavior, product demand, and inventory optimization. Apache Ignite's **machine learning libraries** can be used to train predictive models for various use cases, such as demand forecasting, fraud detection, or recommendation systems. The ability to perform computations directly on in-memory data and distribute the workload across multiple nodes significantly speeds up the training and inference processes, making it ideal for machine learning workflows.

In **telecommunications**, Apache Ignite is employed to handle real-time data processing and analytics for network monitoring and optimization. Telecom companies collect vast amounts of data from network devices, customer interactions, and usage patterns. This data needs to be processed in real-time to detect network failures, prevent service disruptions, and improve customer experiences. Apache Ignite's ability to perform distributed analytics enables telecom providers to process and analyze this data in memory, providing real-time insights into network performance, traffic loads, and customer behavior. Using Apache Ignite in such use cases allows providers to respond to issues faster and optimize their networks dynamically, ensuring better service delivery and reducing operational costs.

In **healthcare**, Apache Ignite is used to handle large-scale medical data and ensure quick access to patient records, diagnostic images, and clinical data. **Electronic health records (EHRs)** and **health information systems (HIS)** rely on fast, reliable access to patient information across multiple healthcare providers. Apache Ignite's in-memory data grid provides the necessary performance and scalability to store and access patient data securely and efficiently. For example, when a doctor or healthcare professional accesses a patient's medical history or diagnostic results, Apache Ignite can quickly retrieve this information from memory, even when the data comes from multiple sources such as lab tests, medical imaging, or prescriptions. This enables healthcare providers to make informed decisions in real-time, improving patient care outcomes and reducing delays in critical treatments.

Financial institutions also leverage Apache Ignite for high-speed transaction processing. In this domain, systems need to handle real-time payments, risk assessments, fraud detection, and credit scoring, all of which require quick and reliable access to large volumes of financial data. Apache Ignite is used as an in-memory processing engine to support these real-time operations. By caching frequently accessed financial data and leveraging Ignite's distributed computing capabilities, financial institutions can process transactions and perform risk assessments more quickly. For example, Ignite can be integrated into **real-time fraud detection systems**, where every transaction is analyzed against predefined patterns to flag suspicious activity. This type of processing requires low-latency, high-throughput capabilities, which Apache Ignite provides.

Another use case for Apache Ignite is in **gaming**, particularly in multiplayer online games that require real-time data processing for player actions, game state updates, and leaderboard management. In online games, it is crucial to update the game state in real-time, process player interactions, and maintain consistency across multiple game servers. Apache Ignite's in-memory data grid is used to store game state and player data, allowing for quick updates and queries to maintain the gaming experience. It can also store the game's leaderboard in memory, ensuring that player rankings are updated instantly as players engage in the game.

Lastly, Apache Ignite is widely used for **enterprise data integration**, where businesses need to integrate and analyze data from multiple disparate systems in real-time. Organizations may have data spread across on-premise systems, cloud platforms, and external databases. Apache

Ignite can serve as a **unified data platform**, pulling together data from various sources, performing real-time analysis, and delivering insights. The **Ignite SQL engine** enables querying across multiple data sources, ensuring that data from legacy systems, modern databases, and even streaming sources can be queried and analyzed together in real-time. This integration capability is particularly useful for **financial institutions**, **retailers**, and **manufacturers** that need to consolidate data for real-time decision-making, performance monitoring, and business intelligence.

Apache Ignite's flexibility and power make it an ideal platform for a wide range of real-world use cases. From **real-time analytics** in financial services and **distributed caching** in e-commerce to **machine learning** in retail and **network monitoring** in telecommunications, Ignite helps organizations process and analyze large datasets at scale with minimal latency. Its ability to integrate with existing systems, deliver high availability, and provide low-latency access to data makes it a critical tool in the modern data-driven landscape. Whether handling massive IoT data streams or optimizing game performance, Apache Ignite is a cornerstone for building responsive, scalable, and fault-tolerant applications.

BOOK 3

ADVANCED CACHING TECHNIQUES
REDIS, MEMCACHED, AND APACHE IGNITE IN PRACTICE

ROB BOTWRIGHT

Chapter 1: Introduction to Advanced Caching Techniques

Advanced caching techniques are crucial for improving application performance by reducing the load on databases, speeding up response times, and enhancing the overall user experience. Caching involves temporarily storing copies of data in memory, making it easily accessible for future requests without the need to access slower data sources such as databases or external APIs. While basic caching can improve performance, advanced caching techniques provide greater control and flexibility, allowing developers to optimize memory usage, handle complex data structures, and implement sophisticated eviction and invalidation strategies. These techniques are particularly important for large-scale systems that need to manage high volumes of data and deliver low-latency responses in real time.

One of the primary advanced caching techniques is **cache partitioning**. In a distributed caching system, cache partitioning divides the cache into smaller, more manageable pieces, called **partitions**, which are then distributed across multiple nodes in a cluster. Each partition contains a subset of the data, and each node is responsible for storing and managing one or more partitions. Partitioning improves scalability, as new nodes can be added to the cluster to handle more data without overloading any single node. This technique helps balance the cache load across the cluster, ensuring that no node becomes a bottleneck. It also allows for **parallelization**, where queries can be executed simultaneously across multiple partitions, significantly reducing query response times for large datasets. Partitioning is especially useful for high-performance applications like **e-commerce platforms**, **financial trading systems**, and **social media applications**, where real-time performance and scalability are critical.

Another important advanced caching technique is **cache replication**. While partitioning divides data across nodes, replication creates multiple copies of the same data and stores them on different nodes. This improves **data availability** and **fault tolerance**, ensuring that if one node fails, another node with a replica of the data can take over without interrupting service. Replication provides **high availability**, as it ensures that the data remains accessible even during node failures. However, it comes with an increased memory cost because each replica consumes additional memory. To optimize replication, developers can configure how many copies of each data item should be maintained, depending on the availability and fault tolerance requirements. In scenarios where the cache must be highly available, such as in **cloud-based applications** or **online banking systems**, cache replication provides the necessary redundancy to maintain uninterrupted service.

Near caching is another advanced technique that helps improve performance, especially for frequently accessed data. In near caching, each node in the system stores a local copy of data that it frequently accesses. This reduces the need for remote data requests, making data retrieval faster for the node, especially in systems with a large distributed cache. By maintaining a **local cache** on each node, near caching minimizes the latency associated with fetching data from other nodes in the cluster. For instance, in a large-scale web application where certain user profiles are frequently queried, near caching can ensure that the user's data is quickly available from the node that the user is interacting with, reducing response times. The **near cache** works in tandem with the global cache, where less frequently accessed data is stored, ensuring that the system remains efficient even as the data set grows. This technique is particularly beneficial in **content delivery networks (CDNs)** and **streaming services**, where quick access to frequently used data is essential for maintaining a smooth user experience.

A related technique is **cache eviction**, which refers to the process of removing data from the cache when memory becomes full or when the data is no longer needed. Advanced eviction strategies help ensure that the most relevant data stays in memory while less important or stale data is removed. One of the most widely used eviction strategies is **Least Recently Used (LRU)**, which evicts the least recently accessed data when space is needed. LRU works under the assumption that data that hasn't been used recently is less likely to be used again in the near future. However, LRU is not always ideal in every situation, and in certain cases, **Least Frequently Used (LFU)** or **Time-to-Live (TTL)** policies might be more effective. LFU evicts data that has been accessed the least over a specified period, ensuring that data with higher access frequency remains in the cache. TTL, on the other hand, automatically evicts data after a specified time period, making it ideal for data that has an expiration date, such as session information or temporary data in **real-time web applications**.

Write-through and **write-behind** caching are two other advanced caching strategies related to **data persistence** and **consistency**. With **write-through caching**, data is written to both the cache and the underlying data store (such as a database) at the same time. This ensures that the cache

134

remains consistent with the source of truth, but it can introduce some performance overhead due to the additional write operation. Write-through caching is ideal for situations where data consistency between the cache and the data store is crucial, such as in **financial systems** or **inventory management** applications. On the other hand, **write-behind caching** writes data to the cache first and then asynchronously writes the data to the underlying data store. This improves write performance by reducing latency, as it does not block the application while waiting for the data store operation to complete. However, write-behind introduces the risk of data inconsistency if the cache and data store become out of sync before the data is written to the store. It is commonly used in **real-time analytics systems** where write performance is critical, and slight data inconsistencies can be tolerated.

Another key technique for advanced caching is **cache invalidation**. Invalidation ensures that stale or outdated data is removed from the cache and replaced with fresh data from the source of truth. This is particularly important in scenarios where data changes frequently and it is essential to reflect the latest updates in the cache. Cache invalidation can be managed in various ways, such as **event-driven invalidation**, where cache entries are automatically invalidated based on changes in the underlying data, or **manual invalidation**, where developers explicitly remove or refresh cache entries. In **e-commerce systems**, for example, invalidating cached product details or pricing information when new stock is added or prices are updated is crucial for maintaining the accuracy of the data shown to users.

Distributed cache coherence is another aspect of advanced caching techniques, which ensures that cache data remains consistent across multiple nodes in a distributed system. In large-scale systems, data can be cached across several nodes, and managing the consistency of that cached data is crucial for maintaining system integrity. Techniques like **replication and partitioning** are used in distributed caches to ensure that changes to cached data are reflected across all nodes, preventing scenarios where different nodes have inconsistent or outdated cache entries. In systems that require high consistency and reliability, such as **cloud applications** or **multinational services**, managing distributed cache coherence ensures that users are always presented with the latest and most accurate data.

As systems continue to scale, advanced caching techniques become essential for ensuring that applications can handle larger volumes of data and more users while maintaining high performance. Techniques like partitioning, replication, near caching, eviction, and invalidation work together to create a flexible, high-performance caching layer that can meet the demands of modern applications. By implementing these advanced strategies, developers can optimize the use of memory, reduce the load on backend systems, and ensure that their applications deliver fast, reliable, and scalable experiences. Whether it's for accelerating data access, managing real-time user sessions, or optimizing complex queries, advanced caching techniques provide the necessary tools to enhance performance in a wide range of applications.

Chapter 2: Deep Dive into Redis: Advanced Features and Use Cases

Redis, an open-source in-memory data structure store, has become one of the most popular tools for high-performance data caching, message brokering, and real-time analytics. While Redis is well-known for its simplicity and speed, it also offers a range of advanced features that allow developers to build highly scalable, fault-tolerant systems. These advanced features make Redis more than just a caching solution, extending its capabilities to complex applications in areas like data storage, message queues, real-time analytics, and even machine learning. A deep dive into Redis's advanced features reveals a wide range of possibilities for building powerful, efficient, and highly responsive applications across many domains.

One of the most powerful features of Redis is its **support for a variety of data types**. While Redis started as a simple key-value store, it has evolved to support more complex data types such as **strings, hashes, lists, sets, sorted sets, bitmaps, hyperloglogs**, and **geospatial indexes**. These data structures offer more flexibility for developers, allowing them to store and manipulate different kinds of data in memory. For example, **sorted sets** provide a way to maintain an ordered collection of elements based on their scores, making it easy to implement features like leaderboards or priority queues. **Hashes** in Redis allow you to store field-value pairs, which is particularly useful for modeling objects in memory, such as storing user profiles or session data. Redis's support for **lists** and **sets** also adds significant value, especially when handling tasks like real-time data streaming or managing unique elements, like a list of users who have interacted with a particular piece of content.

In addition to these fundamental data types, Redis supports advanced features like **transactions** and **pipelining**. **Transactions** in Redis are supported through the **MULTI**, **EXEC**, and **WATCH** commands, which allow developers to execute multiple commands atomically, ensuring consistency within a transaction. Redis transactions provide atomicity, isolation, and consistency, although not full ACID compliance, which is often enough for many use cases, particularly when strict durability is not a requirement. Redis also supports **pipelining**, which enables clients to send multiple commands to the server without waiting for responses. This minimizes the round-trip time for commands and can drastically improve throughput, particularly when handling large numbers of operations simultaneously.

One of the most notable advanced features in Redis is **pub/sub** (publish/subscribe), which enables real-time messaging between clients. Redis's pub/sub mechanism allows one client to **publish** messages to a specific **channel**, while other clients can **subscribe** to that channel to receive updates. This feature is ideal for real-time applications, such as chat applications, live notifications, or event-driven systems, where multiple clients need to receive data instantly as it changes. The pub/sub feature in Redis is simple to implement, fast, and scalable, making it a popular choice for systems that require low-latency communication. It also scales well in distributed environments, where messages can be propagated to subscribers across multiple Redis nodes.

Persistence is another key advanced feature in Redis that helps ensure data durability while maintaining the high performance expected of an in-memory store. Redis offers two persistence options: **RDB (Redis Database) snapshots** and **AOF (Append-Only File)**. RDB snapshots create point-in-time backups of the dataset, which are stored on disk. These snapshots can be taken at regular intervals or based on changes to the dataset. The AOF persistence option logs every write operation to an append-only file, providing more granular durability, as every change to the data is captured. AOF is more durable than RDB, but it introduces some overhead, as write operations are logged before being executed. Redis also provides the option to combine RDB and AOF, offering a hybrid approach that balances performance with data durability. Redis's persistence mechanisms are essential in environments where durability is important but where the system still needs to handle massive workloads with low latency.

In terms of **high availability and fault tolerance**, Redis offers **Replication** and **Redis Sentinel** for managing distributed Redis setups. Redis replication allows data to be copied across multiple Redis instances, ensuring that if one node fails, others can take over, providing high availability. Redis Sentinel is a system used to manage Redis clusters and automatically handle **failover** in the event of node failures. It monitors Redis servers and promotes a slave server to a master server when the master fails, allowing the system to continue running without manual intervention. Sentinel provides automated failover and configuration management, helping ensure that Redis remains available and resilient to failures, even in large, distributed environments.

Another important Redis feature is its **cluster mode**, which enables horizontal scaling by partitioning the data across multiple Redis nodes. Redis Cluster provides a distributed architecture where data is divided into **hash slots**, and each node is responsible for a subset of these slots. The cluster can automatically redistribute data across nodes when the cluster expands or contracts, ensuring a balanced load. Redis Cluster supports **automatic failover**, so if one node fails, the cluster can promote a replica to take its place. This feature is essential for applications that require large-scale distributed caching, as it allows Redis to scale out across many nodes while maintaining high performance and fault tolerance.

Redis also provides **geospatial capabilities**, which enable developers to store and query geospatial data, such as location coordinates, within Redis. Redis's **geospatial indexing** allows users to store data like the longitude and latitude of geographic locations and perform queries to find distances between points, or retrieve all locations within a certain radius. This is especially useful for applications like ride-sharing services, where finding the nearest cars to users is a frequent and time-sensitive operation. Redis's geospatial commands, such as **GEODIST**, **GEORADIUS**, and **GEOHASH**, make it easy to store and query geospatial data in memory at blazing fast speeds.

For use cases that require **advanced analytics** and **counting** operations, Redis provides features like **HyperLogLog** and **Bitmaps**. **HyperLogLog** is a probabilistic data structure that allows Redis to count unique items in a set with minimal memory overhead. It is particularly useful for estimating the cardinality of large sets, such as counting unique visitors to a website, without requiring a lot of memory. **Bitmaps** are another compact data structure in Redis, useful for representing binary data or tracking the presence of items. Bitmaps allow developers to efficiently store and manipulate large datasets of binary values, such as user activity flags, making them highly suitable for applications in areas like **user engagement tracking** or **clickstream analysis**.

Redis also includes a powerful **Lua scripting engine**, which allows developers to execute custom logic atomically within Redis. Lua scripts can be executed as part of Redis commands, enabling more complex operations that can be executed on the server side, without needing to transfer large amounts of data between the client and the server. By using Lua scripts, developers can perform operations like **conditional updates**, **batch processing**, or **aggregating data** within Redis, reducing the overhead of sending multiple commands and improving performance.

One of the newer features of Redis is **RedisAI**, a module that integrates machine learning capabilities into Redis. RedisAI allows models to be run directly in Redis, enabling the use of pre-trained machine learning models for real-time inference. This integration is particularly useful for applications that require low-latency predictions, such as recommendation systems, fraud detection, and personalization engines. RedisAI supports popular machine learning frameworks like TensorFlow, PyTorch, and ONNX, making it easy to deploy models and perform inference directly within Redis.

Redis's advanced features, including its support for multiple data types, transactions, persistence, high availability, clustering, geospatial data, and machine learning, make it a highly versatile platform for a wide range of applications. Whether you need a high-speed cache, a messaging system, or an in-memory database, Redis offers a comprehensive suite of tools that can be adapted to meet the performance and scalability needs of modern applications. From real-time analytics in finance and e-commerce to machine learning in AI-powered services, Redis empowers developers to build fast, resilient, and scalable systems capable of handling demanding workloads at scale.

Chapter 3: Memcached Beyond the Basics: Performance and Scalability

Memcached is one of the most widely used open-source, high-performance, distributed memory object caching systems that helps reduce database load and improve application response times. While Memcached is typically used for basic caching, it offers many advanced features and configuration options that go beyond its basic functionality, allowing it to be effectively used for large-scale applications with high-performance and scalability requirements. Understanding how to optimize Memcached for performance and scalability is crucial for ensuring that it can handle growing workloads and data demands while maintaining low latency and high throughput.

One of the first aspects to consider when aiming to improve **Memcached performance** is memory management. Memcached stores data in RAM, and the amount of memory allocated to Memcached directly impacts its performance. By default, Memcached allocates memory based on the system's available RAM, but tuning the memory allocation for specific use cases is often necessary. For example, if Memcached is being used to store session data or frequently accessed database query results, allocating sufficient memory to the system is critical to prevent frequent evictions, which occur when Memcached runs out of memory and starts removing data to make space for new entries. Optimizing the memory settings for Memcached by adjusting the -m flag (which defines the maximum amount of memory) based on workload patterns helps prevent such evictions and ensures that data stays in memory, providing faster access times and reducing system overhead.

Another key factor in Memcached's performance is its **eviction policy**. Memcached uses an **LRU (Least Recently Used)** eviction algorithm by default, where the least recently accessed items are evicted first when the system runs out of memory. However, this is just one approach to managing memory utilization. The LRU policy is useful for most use cases, but in certain situations, developers might need to adjust eviction strategies based on the type of data being stored. For example, **least frequently used (LFU)** or **random eviction** strategies might be more appropriate in specific scenarios where certain items need to be kept in the cache even if they haven't been recently accessed. By understanding the different eviction policies and applying the most appropriate one, you can optimize how data is removed from memory and ensure that critical data is not evicted prematurely.

Multi-threading support is another important aspect that enhances Memcached's performance. Earlier versions of Memcached operated with a single thread, which limited its ability to scale effectively on multi-core systems. In later versions, Memcached introduced multi-threading support, allowing it to leverage modern multi-core processors more effectively. By enabling multi-threading, Memcached can handle multiple requests simultaneously, significantly improving its throughput and reducing the time taken to handle concurrent operations. Configuring the number of threads based on the number of CPU cores available on the machine allows Memcached to fully utilize system resources and maintain optimal performance even under heavy load conditions. However, it's important to balance the number of threads with the available memory and network resources to prevent over-utilization of system resources.

For **scalability**, Memcached provides **sharding** capabilities, which allow data to be distributed across multiple Memcached instances, or **nodes**, in a cluster. Sharding helps Memcached handle larger datasets by distributing the cache across multiple servers. Each node in a Memcached cluster holds a portion of the overall data, and data is accessed based on a consistent hashing mechanism that ensures that each request is directed to the correct server. Sharding can be particularly beneficial in large-scale applications where a single Memcached instance would not have enough memory to store all the required data. By spreading data across multiple nodes, Memcached can scale horizontally to handle more traffic, memory, and workload, making it an excellent solution for cloud-based applications or services that experience fluctuating or high-demand traffic patterns.

Another feature that enhances **scalability** is **replication**. Memcached supports replication in the form of **mcrouter**, a high-performance router that provides an abstraction layer for sharded Memcached clusters. Mcrouter allows developers to set up **read replicas**, which are copies of the Memcached data stored across different nodes. These replicas are used to distribute read requests, improving **read throughput** and ensuring that the system remains responsive under high-demand situations. By replicating data across multiple nodes and balancing requests between primary and replica nodes, Memcached can provide better availability and higher throughput. Replication is particularly useful in scenarios where read-heavy workloads need to be efficiently distributed without placing additional pressure on the primary node.

The **consistent hashing** algorithm used in Memcached's sharding and replication mechanisms is a key component for ensuring that the data is evenly distributed across the nodes in the cluster. Consistent hashing helps reduce the likelihood of hotspots, where certain nodes might be overloaded with requests while others are underutilized. This load balancing ensures that requests are evenly spread across all available nodes, improving overall system performance and resource utilization. When a new node is added or removed from the cluster, consistent hashing ensures minimal data reshuffling, avoiding the need to redistribute large amounts of data, which can result in latency spikes. This minimizes the overhead of scaling out the cluster and helps keep the system running smoothly even during rebalancing operations.

Network performance is another critical factor when optimizing Memcached for scalability. Memcached relies heavily on network communication to handle requests between clients and servers, and the performance of the underlying network can significantly impact its efficiency. To maximize network throughput, Memcached can be configured to use **TCP** or **UDP** for communication. TCP ensures reliable transmission of data but may introduce additional overhead due to the need for handshakes and acknowledgments. On the other hand, UDP can provide faster performance by reducing network overhead, though it sacrifices reliability. For high-throughput applications that do not require the level of reliability that TCP provides, switching to UDP can reduce latency and improve performance. It is important to ensure that network bandwidth is sufficient to handle the volume of requests Memcached will receive, especially in large-scale distributed deployments.

Compression is another optimization technique that can be used to improve Memcached performance, particularly when dealing with large objects that need to be cached. Compressing data before storing it in Memcached reduces memory usage, allowing more data to fit within the allocated memory, thereby increasing the cache hit ratio and reducing the frequency of database lookups. While compression can introduce some computational overhead, the benefits of reduced memory usage often outweigh the trade-offs. Compression techniques, such as **Zlib**, can be integrated into Memcached, enabling more efficient use of memory resources, especially when caching large datasets like images, videos, or JSON objects.

Finally, **monitoring and tuning** are essential for maintaining optimal performance in Memcached. Monitoring tools such as **Memcached's stats command** provide real-time insights into the health of the system, including key performance metrics like cache hit/miss ratio, memory usage, eviction rates, and command processing time. By tracking these metrics, administrators can identify bottlenecks, understand data access patterns, and fine-tune the system for optimal performance.

Regular monitoring allows for quick identification of issues such as memory overflows or high eviction rates, which can negatively impact performance. By adjusting configuration settings based on real-time data, such as tuning the memory allocation or adjusting eviction policies, administrators can ensure that Memcached operates efficiently at scale.

By optimizing Memcached's memory management, eviction strategies, network performance, and clustering capabilities, developers can ensure that Memcached performs optimally in large-scale, high-demand applications. When configured correctly, Memcached can provide exceptional performance and scalability, handling millions of requests per second while maintaining low-latency access to data. Whether used for caching, session management, or real-time analytics, Memcached is a powerful tool for building fast, scalable systems that meet the performance needs of modern applications.

Chapter 4: Apache Ignite: Leveraging In-Memory Data Grids for Caching

Apache Ignite is an open-source, distributed in-memory computing platform that provides powerful features for caching and in-memory data processing. It leverages the concept of an **in-memory data grid (IMDG)** to store and manage data in memory across a distributed cluster of nodes, allowing for incredibly fast access and high throughput. By utilizing an in-memory data grid, Apache Ignite can significantly reduce latency and increase the speed of applications that require frequent data access, such as real-time analytics, financial services, e-commerce platforms, and IoT applications. In this context, **caching** becomes a fundamental part of Apache Ignite's functionality, enabling systems to store data in memory and retrieve it at lightning-fast speeds without relying on slower disk-based storage.

One of the core advantages of Apache Ignite is its **distributed nature**, which allows the caching layer to scale horizontally by adding more nodes to the cluster. This **distributed cache** ensures that data is spread across multiple nodes, enabling high availability and fault tolerance while preventing any single node from becoming a bottleneck. Data is partitioned across the cluster, with each partition stored on multiple nodes for redundancy. This ensures that even if one node goes down, another node with a replica of the data can take over without affecting the system's overall performance. The **distributed in-memory cache** that Apache Ignite provides is designed to handle high volumes of data while maintaining low-latency access, making it ideal for use cases where real-time data access is crucial.

A key feature of Apache Ignite's caching capabilities is its **cache partitioning** model. Data is divided into partitions and distributed across the nodes in the cluster. Each partition is managed by a specific node, and Apache Ignite ensures that data is distributed evenly across the cluster to avoid overloading any single node. This model provides scalability, as more nodes can be added to handle increasing data volumes. The partitioning mechanism in Apache Ignite uses **affinity** to ensure that related data items are stored on the same node or on nodes that are close to each other in the network. This reduces the need for remote calls, improving performance by ensuring that data can be accessed locally whenever possible.

In addition to partitioning, Apache Ignite provides **cache replication**, which ensures high availability by maintaining copies of data across multiple nodes in the cluster. Replication is particularly important for fault tolerance, as it allows data to be available even in the event of node failures. Apache Ignite supports configurable replication policies, where data can be replicated across a specified number of nodes, ensuring that the cache remains available regardless of failures. By using replication, Ignite can provide stronger guarantees of data availability, ensuring that even if a node goes down, the data is still accessible from another node in the cluster. This approach is essential for applications that require 24/7 availability, such as online banking, e-commerce websites, or healthcare systems.

Another important aspect of Apache Ignite's caching functionality is **cache eviction**. As memory resources are finite, it is essential to have strategies for evicting old or infrequently used data to make room for new data. Apache Ignite supports multiple eviction strategies, including **Least Recently Used (LRU)**, **Least Frequently Used (LFU)**, and **Random Eviction**. These strategies determine which data to evict when the cache reaches its memory limit. The **LRU eviction policy** evicts the least recently accessed data, assuming that data that hasn't been used recently is less likely to be used again soon. The **LFU eviction policy** evicts the least frequently accessed data, ensuring that the most commonly accessed data remains in the cache. The eviction policy can be configured based on the requirements of the specific application, allowing for greater control over cache behavior. For example, in a system that handles user sessions, the eviction strategy could prioritize retaining the most active user sessions while removing data from inactive sessions.

Near caching is another advanced caching feature offered by Apache Ignite, which helps improve the performance of frequently accessed data. In **near caching**, each node in the cluster maintains a local copy of the data that it accesses most often. This local cache reduces the need to access remote nodes, improving response times for frequently accessed data. Near caching is particularly useful in systems with high data locality, where certain data items are accessed more often by specific nodes in the cluster. For example, in a content delivery network (CDN), where users frequently request content from the same geographical region, near caching allows data to be cached locally on the edge nodes, reducing latency and improving content delivery speed. By storing commonly accessed data on the node that requests it, near caching helps minimize the need for inter-node communication, resulting in faster data access.

In addition to **local caching** and **near caching**, Apache Ignite provides support for **distributed SQL queries** over the cached data, allowing developers to run complex queries directly on the data stored in memory. Ignite's **SQL engine** is fully integrated with the in-memory data grid, enabling users to perform distributed SQL queries across the cluster without needing to rely on external databases. This capability allows for real-time analytics and querying of data in the cache, enabling businesses to derive insights instantly without the latency associated with traditional disk-based databases. Apache Ignite supports SQL queries using standard ANSI SQL syntax, making it easy for developers to interact with the data in a familiar and efficient way. The ability to run distributed SQL queries on in-memory data means that businesses can make decisions quickly, even when dealing with large datasets.

Persistence is another key feature of Apache Ignite's caching architecture. While in-memory caching is fast and efficient, it may not be sufficient for use cases that require data durability. Apache Ignite offers **persistence** options that allow data to be written to disk while still providing in-memory performance. Ignite's persistence mechanisms include **RDB snapshots** and **AOF (Append-Only File)** logging. The RDB snapshot mechanism allows Ignite to take periodic snapshots of the data in memory and save it to disk, ensuring that data can be recovered in the event of a failure. AOF logging records every write operation to disk, providing a more durable option for data persistence. These persistence options allow Ignite to deliver the performance benefits of in-memory caching while maintaining data durability for applications that require it.

For more advanced use cases, Apache Ignite can also integrate with external systems, including databases, message queues, and big data platforms. By acting as a distributed cache between the application and backend systems, Apache Ignite helps to reduce the load on databases and improve the overall performance of the system. For example, in an e-commerce system, Apache Ignite can cache frequently requested product information, reducing the number of queries to the underlying database. Integration with **Apache Kafka** or **Apache Spark** allows Ignite to act as a real-time data processing engine, making it suitable for applications that require high-speed data ingestion and real-time analytics, such as fraud detection, sensor data processing, and predictive analytics.

Apache Ignite's ability to **scale horizontally** and handle large-scale, distributed caching workloads makes it an ideal solution for applications with demanding data access requirements. By using **in-memory data grids** for caching, Apache Ignite provides low-latency data access, high availability, fault tolerance, and scalability. Whether used for simple caching scenarios, real-time analytics, or large-scale data processing, Apache Ignite helps businesses improve performance and ensure that applications remain responsive even under heavy load conditions. Its flexibility, performance, and ease of integration make it a powerful tool for building modern, high-performance applications that require fast, reliable access to data.

Chapter 5: Data Sharding and Partitioning in Distributed Caching Systems

Data sharding and partitioning are essential concepts in distributed caching systems that enable large-scale applications to efficiently manage, store, and retrieve data across multiple nodes or servers. Both strategies are designed to break down data into smaller chunks, distribute these chunks across various nodes, and balance the load between different servers. The main goal of sharding and partitioning is to improve performance, scalability, and fault tolerance while reducing bottlenecks and ensuring high availability. These techniques are particularly useful in modern, high-traffic applications, where a single server would be unable to handle the large amounts of data and high request rates required by users. As such, data sharding and partitioning play a crucial role in the efficiency of distributed caching systems, making them scalable and capable of handling huge datasets.

Sharding refers to the process of dividing data into smaller, more manageable pieces called **shards**, which are then distributed across multiple nodes in a cluster. Each shard contains a subset of the data and is managed by a specific node in the cluster. The goal of sharding is to ensure that no single node is responsible for handling all the data or processing all the requests, thus distributing the workload evenly across the cluster. The **sharding key**, often based on the data itself, determines how the data is distributed. For instance, in an e-commerce application, data related to products could be sharded based on the product ID, where products with similar IDs are stored together on the same node. This ensures that related data can be accessed quickly and efficiently without requiring extensive data transfers across nodes.

Data partitioning is a closely related concept to sharding, but it focuses more on how data is distributed across different nodes within the system. While sharding divides data into smaller units and assigns each unit to a specific node, partitioning ensures that data within each partition is stored and accessed efficiently. Partitioning can be based on different strategies, such as **range-based partitioning** or **hash-based partitioning**. In **range-based partitioning**, data is split into contiguous ranges, with each range being stored on a different node. For example, in a user management system, users could be partitioned by their user IDs, with one partition containing users with IDs from 1 to 1000, another containing IDs from 1001 to 2000, and so on. On the other hand, **hash-based partitioning** divides data based on a hash function applied to the sharding key. The hash function ensures that data is evenly distributed across all nodes, which helps balance the load and improve system performance.

Both **sharding** and **partitioning** allow distributed caching systems to scale horizontally, meaning they can handle increasing data volumes and user requests simply by adding more nodes to the cluster. When more nodes are added, the data can be re-partitioned or re-sharded to maintain an even distribution, ensuring that no node is overwhelmed. This scaling capability is crucial for modern applications, where user demands can fluctuate significantly. Horizontal scaling allows distributed caching systems to accommodate sudden spikes in traffic, such as during holiday sales for an e-commerce site or when new features are rolled out in a social media application.

To manage the distribution and rebalancing of data, many distributed caching systems use **consistent hashing**. Consistent hashing ensures that data is distributed evenly across the nodes in the system while minimizing the need for data redistribution when nodes are added or removed. This hashing technique involves assigning a **hash value** to each piece of data based on its sharding key and then mapping the data to a virtual ring of nodes. When a new node is added to the system, only a small subset of the data needs to be moved to the new node, minimizing the impact on the rest of the system and preventing large-scale data reshuffling. This approach enhances the efficiency of both sharding and partitioning in distributed caching systems and helps ensure that the system can scale without significant overhead.

One of the challenges with data sharding and partitioning is managing **data locality**. Data locality refers to the concept of storing related data on the same node or on nodes that are close to each other in the network. By ensuring that related data is placed together, the system can minimize the need for cross-node communication, which can introduce latency and slow down performance. For instance, in a distributed caching system, if a user's profile data and their recent activity logs are stored on different nodes, every time the profile data is accessed, the system will need to make a network call to fetch the activity logs from another node. By using **affinity** and intelligent partitioning schemes, distributed caching systems can ensure that related data is co-located on the same node, improving performance by reducing remote calls.

Replication is another important concept in distributed caching systems that works hand-in-hand with sharding and partitioning. Replication involves creating multiple copies of the data on different nodes, ensuring that the data remains available even in the event of a node failure. In a distributed cache, data is typically **replicated across nodes** to provide **fault tolerance** and improve data availability. When data is replicated, the system ensures that if a node goes down, the replicated data on another node can be used without causing downtime. This is particularly important for systems that require high availability, such as those used in e-commerce, banking, or social media platforms. However, while replication improves fault tolerance, it can also increase the memory and network overhead because each piece of data must be stored on multiple nodes.

Cache consistency is a critical concern when dealing with sharding and partitioning in distributed caching systems. Since data is distributed across multiple nodes, maintaining consistency between the cached data and the source of truth (e.g., a database) can become challenging. Several strategies exist to ensure that cached data remains consistent with the underlying database. One common approach is **cache invalidation**, where the cache is cleared or updated when the underlying data changes. This can be done either **event-driven** or by using **time-to-live (TTL)** policies, where data is removed from the cache after a specified period. Another strategy is **write-through**

caching, where updates to the cache are immediately written to the database, ensuring that the cache always reflects the most recent data. **Read-through caching** is another technique where data is fetched from the cache first, and if it's not present, it is retrieved from the database and then stored in the cache for future access.

Handling **data consistency** across partitions and shards requires careful consideration of the trade-offs between **eventual consistency** and **strong consistency**. In scenarios where absolute consistency is necessary, strong consistency protocols like **two-phase commit (2PC)** or **Paxos** can be employed to ensure that updates to multiple nodes are applied atomically. However, in many applications, eventual consistency is sufficient, and distributed caching systems can leverage techniques like **quorum-based reads and writes** to ensure that data is eventually consistent across all replicas while optimizing for performance and availability.

When implementing **data sharding and partitioning**, it is also essential to monitor the **load distribution** across the nodes in the cluster. An imbalance in load can lead to performance degradation, as some nodes may become overloaded while others are underutilized. Tools for monitoring cluster health, such as **Apache Ignite's** built-in monitoring and **Prometheus** integration, can help detect these imbalances and guide decisions about scaling the cluster or redistributing data. By actively managing the distribution of data and adjusting to changing traffic patterns, distributed caching systems can maintain high performance even as workloads grow and evolve.

Data sharding and partitioning are foundational components of any distributed caching system, enabling horizontal scalability, load balancing, and high availability. These techniques, combined with intelligent partitioning strategies, data locality optimization, and replication, allow distributed caching systems to handle large volumes of data and traffic while maintaining performance and reliability. As systems grow in size and complexity, understanding and managing sharding and partitioning becomes critical for maintaining efficient, high-performing applications. By leveraging these concepts, businesses can ensure that their distributed caching systems are scalable, fault-tolerant, and able to meet the demands of modern, data-driven applications.

Chapter 6: Managing Cache Eviction and Expiration Strategies

Managing cache eviction and expiration strategies is an essential aspect of optimizing the performance of caching systems, particularly when dealing with large datasets or high-traffic applications. In-memory caching solutions, such as **Memcached** and **Apache Ignite**, rely heavily on eviction and expiration policies to ensure that the cache remains effective and efficient over time. These strategies determine how data is removed from the cache, either when the cache reaches its memory limit or when cached data is no longer valid or useful. Properly configuring these policies is critical to maintaining the system's performance, ensuring that frequently accessed data remains available while minimizing the use of resources for stale or irrelevant data.

Cache eviction refers to the process of removing data from the cache when it is no longer needed or when space is required for new data. Since memory is finite, eviction policies are necessary to control which data should be removed first. Different eviction strategies can be applied depending on the use case and application requirements. One of the most common eviction strategies is **Least Recently Used (LRU)**, which removes the least recently accessed data when the cache is full. The idea behind LRU is that data that hasn't been accessed recently is less likely to be accessed again in the near future, making it a prime candidate for eviction. This strategy works well in scenarios where the cache contains a mix of data, and the most frequently used data is expected to be accessed again shortly. However, LRU eviction can introduce overhead in tracking access patterns, particularly when managing large datasets, which may make it less effective in some cases.

Another popular eviction strategy is **Least Frequently Used (LFU)**, which evicts the data that has been accessed the least over a given period. LFU is more sophisticated than LRU because it not only considers the recentness of access but also how often a given piece of data has been accessed. This can be especially beneficial for applications where certain data is frequently accessed over long periods, and the goal is to retain the most valuable or popular data. For example, in a **recommendation engine**, data related to popular items may be accessed repeatedly, and retaining that data in the cache improves overall system efficiency. However, LFU also has its drawbacks, particularly the complexity of tracking frequency counts for each cache entry, which can introduce performance overhead in high-volume systems.

Random eviction is another eviction policy that may be used in cases where more sophisticated strategies like LRU or LFU are too complex or unnecessary. In random eviction, when the cache reaches its memory limit, data is randomly chosen for removal. This strategy can be effective in systems where data access patterns are unpredictable or where the cache is being used to store transient data that does not require frequent access. The randomness of the eviction process ensures that no single data point is favored, which can be beneficial when there is no clear pattern in data access. However, the downside is that valuable data might be evicted arbitrarily, potentially causing more cache misses and reduced cache hit rates.

Time-to-Live (TTL) is a commonly used expiration strategy, which involves setting an expiration time for each cached item. When the TTL is reached, the cached data is considered stale and is automatically removed from the cache. TTL is particularly useful when caching data that has a limited useful lifespan, such as session data, authentication tokens, or temporary results from API calls. By setting appropriate TTL values, the system ensures that the cache does not become bloated with stale data, which could otherwise consume unnecessary memory and reduce performance. TTL values can be set globally for all cache entries or individually, depending on the nature of the data. In scenarios where real-time accuracy is important, the TTL can be set to a shorter duration to ensure that data is regularly refreshed, but for less time-sensitive data, longer TTLs might be appropriate.

In addition to TTL, **sliding expiration** is another expiration strategy that allows data to stay in the cache as long as it is actively used. With sliding expiration, the TTL resets each time the data is accessed. This ensures that frequently accessed data remains in the cache, while less frequently accessed data is eventually evicted when the cache reaches its memory limit. Sliding expiration is useful in situations where it is important to keep data in memory for as long as it is actively needed, such as user sessions or high-priority data in an e-commerce application. However, it requires proper tracking of access timestamps and can lead to unpredictable cache sizes, especially in systems with erratic usage patterns.

Cache invalidation is another important aspect of cache management, particularly when dealing with **data consistency**. In a distributed caching system, invalidating data ensures that any changes to the underlying data source are reflected in the cache. Without cache invalidation, there is a risk of serving outdated or incorrect data from the cache, leading to inconsistencies and unreliable system behavior. Cache invalidation can occur in several ways. **Event-driven invalidation** is one method, where the cache is notified of changes to the underlying data source and invalidates or refreshes the relevant cache entries. This can be done through message queues or database triggers that notify the cache when updates occur. **Time-based invalidation** is another method, where data in the cache is automatically invalidated after a certain period, based on its TTL or other expiration criteria. This is useful when exact consistency isn't required, and the data is likely to change periodically.

Managing cache eviction and expiration strategies in a distributed environment adds an extra layer of complexity. Distributed systems must ensure that evictions and expirations are synchronized across multiple nodes, as each node may hold different portions of the cached data. This is particularly important in **sharded caching systems**, where data is distributed across several nodes, and consistent eviction policies need to be applied uniformly. For instance, if a cache entry expires on one node, other nodes in the system must be aware of this expiration to avoid serving stale data. In some systems, a

distributed cache coherence protocol may be implemented to maintain consistency across all cache nodes and ensure that data is properly synchronized.

Another important consideration when managing cache eviction and expiration strategies is **cache pre-warming**. Pre-warming involves loading frequently accessed data into the cache ahead of time, ensuring that cache misses are minimized during high-traffic periods. This is especially useful in applications that experience predictable traffic spikes, such as during **Black Friday** sales or the launch of a new product. By pre-warming the cache with relevant data, the system ensures that critical data is already available in memory, reducing the need to query the database and speeding up response times. Pre-warming can be achieved through periodic cache updates or by using **warm-up scripts** that load essential data into the cache before it is needed.

As applications scale and data access patterns become more complex, managing cache eviction and expiration effectively becomes a balancing act. It requires careful consideration of the trade-offs between data freshness, memory usage, and system performance. By choosing the appropriate eviction policies, expiration strategies, and invalidation mechanisms, developers can create caching systems that deliver high performance while ensuring data consistency and reliability. Properly tuned cache eviction and expiration strategies are crucial to building scalable, efficient, and fault-tolerant distributed systems that meet the demands of modern, data-intensive applications.

Chapter 7: Integrating Redis, Memcached, and Apache Ignite for Hybrid Caching Solutions

Integrating Redis, Memcached, and Apache Ignite for hybrid caching solutions allows organizations to take advantage of the unique features and strengths of each caching technology, creating a highly flexible, scalable, and efficient caching infrastructure. Each of these tools—Redis, Memcached, and Apache Ignite—provides different advantages depending on the specific needs of an application. By leveraging these technologies together, companies can optimize their caching strategies, balancing performance, scalability, and data consistency across multiple use cases. Hybrid caching solutions combine the strengths of these tools to address the complex challenges that arise when building modern, high-performance applications that require low-latency, high-throughput access to data.

Redis, Memcached, and Apache Ignite all operate as in-memory data stores, but their design principles and use cases can vary significantly. Redis is an advanced key-value store that supports complex data types like strings, lists, sets, and hashes, as well as specialized features like **pub/sub** messaging and **geospatial indexing**. Redis also provides strong persistence options through RDB snapshots and append-only file (AOF) logging, allowing it to provide data durability while maintaining high performance. **Memcached**, on the other hand, is a simpler, high-performance caching layer that stores data as key-value pairs and is designed primarily for in-memory caching with **no persistence**. It excels in scenarios where high-speed caching of relatively simple objects is needed, such as caching session data or query results. **Apache Ignite** is an in-memory computing platform with a focus on distributed data grids, SQL querying, and machine learning. It supports partitioned and replicated caches, real-time analytics, and can scale horizontally by adding more nodes to the cluster. Ignite provides a **highly durable** and scalable solution for handling large volumes of data with the ability to perform complex computations on the data stored in memory.

By integrating Redis, Memcached, and Apache Ignite into a hybrid caching solution, organizations can take advantage of each system's strengths. For example, Redis can be used as a high-performance caching layer for applications requiring complex data types, pub/sub messaging, or real-time analytics. Memcached can be utilized for simple, high-throughput caching of session data or short-lived objects that do not require persistence. Apache Ignite, with its **distributed data grid** and advanced querying capabilities, can be used to handle large-scale data caching and analytics, ensuring that complex queries and computations can be performed efficiently in memory.

One common hybrid approach is to **use Memcached as the first layer of caching**, providing a lightweight, fast-access cache for simple key-value data. Memcached's minimalistic design ensures that data can be retrieved with low latency, and since it doesn't store data persistently, it provides high-throughput performance for short-lived data that doesn't need to be preserved after a system restart. Memcached is also highly effective in applications where the same data is requested repeatedly, such as frequently accessed database query results or static resources, as it helps reduce the load on the backend system.

Redis can be used as the **second layer of caching**, handling more complex data structures that require advanced features like lists, sets, hashes, and geospatial data. Redis also supports more sophisticated **persistence** options such as snapshots and AOF logs, making it suitable for use cases that require data durability while maintaining the speed and performance of in-memory data. For example, Redis can be used to cache user session data, configurations, or real-time counters, which are important to keep consistent across restarts. Additionally, Redis' **pub/sub** capabilities make it an excellent choice for applications that require real-time messaging or notifications, such as chat applications, live notifications, or event-driven architectures.

Finally, **Apache Ignite** can be leveraged as the **third layer**, providing a scalable and fault-tolerant solution for large-scale data storage and computation. Apache Ignite's distributed data grid allows for **partitioned** and **replicated caches**, ensuring that data is highly available and can scale horizontally as more nodes are added to the cluster. For applications that require **complex queries**, **real-time analytics**, or **machine learning** models running in-memory, Apache Ignite offers the ability to perform these operations at high speed without having to access disk storage. For instance, Apache Ignite can store customer data, analytics results, or transaction histories, while also supporting SQL queries and machine learning algorithms. Apache Ignite's ability to execute distributed SQL queries on in-memory data enables businesses to perform real-time data analytics and decision-making without the latency of traditional databases.

In a hybrid caching solution, data can be passed between Memcached, Redis, and Apache Ignite based on the specific needs of the application. For example, a multi-tier caching solution might use **Memcached for the initial cache layer** to handle simple, low-latency lookups of frequently accessed data. When more complex data structures or persistence are required, the data can be passed to **Redis**, which handles more advanced operations and ensures that the data is available across application restarts. If the data becomes larger or requires complex analytics or queries, it can be offloaded to **Apache Ignite**, where distributed computation and SQL querying can be performed efficiently.

One key consideration when integrating these three caching technologies is ensuring **data consistency** and **coherence** across the layers. Since each caching layer may store a subset of the data, it is crucial to design a system that ensures that updates to data in one layer are reflected in the others when necessary. This is particularly important in use cases where the data has a short lifespan or is highly dynamic, such as user sessions or real-time user activity. A common approach is to use **cache invalidation** or **cache synchronization mechanisms** to ensure that when data is modified in one cache, it is invalidated or updated in the others, maintaining consistency across the system. These mechanisms can be implemented through **event-driven notifications** or **write-through caching**, where each write operation is first applied to the cache and then to the backend data store.

Another challenge when integrating Redis, Memcached, and Apache Ignite is managing **cache eviction policies**. Each caching system may implement different eviction strategies, such as **Least Recently Used (LRU)**, **Least Frequently Used (LFU)**, or **TTL-based expiration**, and ensuring that the caches operate efficiently without evicting critical data prematurely requires careful configuration. For example, Memcached might handle lightweight data with short TTLs, while Redis could store longer-lived data with more sophisticated eviction rules. Apache Ignite, as a distributed data grid, may handle larger datasets with more robust replication and partitioning strategies. The key to successful integration lies in choosing the appropriate eviction policies for each layer, depending on the type of data being cached and the application's requirements for performance and consistency.

Monitoring and **logging** are also crucial in a hybrid caching solution. Since data is being handled by multiple caching layers, tracking the health and performance of each system is essential for identifying bottlenecks and ensuring smooth operation. Tools like **Prometheus**, **Grafana**, and **Datadog** can be used to monitor the performance of Redis, Memcached, and Apache Ignite, providing real-time insights into cache hit/miss rates, memory usage, and latency. Logging can help track cache interactions across the layers and ensure that data is being transferred correctly, and invalidation or synchronization mechanisms are functioning properly.

In addition to performance monitoring, it is also important to design for **fault tolerance** and **high availability** in a hybrid caching solution. Apache Ignite and Redis both support **replication** and **failover** mechanisms, while Memcached can be integrated with tools like **mcrouter** to enable automated failover. Ensuring that data remains available even in the event of node failures is critical for mission-critical applications. By combining the failover and replication capabilities of all three caching systems, organizations can build highly available, fault-tolerant caching infrastructures that ensure continuous operation even in the face of hardware or software failures.

Integrating Redis, Memcached, and Apache Ignite into a hybrid caching solution provides a flexible, high-performance approach to managing data at scale. By leveraging the strengths of each system, organizations can optimize caching strategies to meet the specific demands of their applications, whether it's for session management, real-time analytics, or complex computations. This approach allows for better scalability, lower latency, and improved availability, making it a powerful strategy for building modern, data-intensive applications.

Chapter 8: Optimizing Cache Performance: Tuning Redis, Memcached, and Ignite

Optimizing cache performance is a critical aspect of building high-performance, distributed systems, particularly when using tools like Redis, Memcached, and Apache Ignite. These in-memory data stores offer powerful caching solutions, but to fully leverage their potential, fine-tuning their configuration and performance settings is essential. By carefully managing how data is stored, accessed, and evicted, organizations can achieve significant improvements in speed, scalability, and resource utilization. Redis, Memcached, and Apache Ignite each have unique features and tuning parameters that, when optimized, can reduce latency, increase throughput, and enhance overall system performance.

For **Redis**, one of the most common optimization strategies is related to memory management. Redis operates entirely in memory, which means that how memory is allocated, used, and managed directly impacts performance. Redis allows administrators to set the **maxmemory** configuration, which limits the amount of memory that Redis can use. When Redis reaches this limit, it will begin evicting data according to the configured eviction policy. The most common eviction policies include **LRU (Least Recently Used), LFU (Least Frequently Used),** and **volatile-ttl**. The **LRU policy** is generally well-suited for caching workloads, as it evicts the least recently accessed data, which is often the least useful. However, when working with high-throughput applications, using the **LFU**

policy may be more beneficial in cases where certain data needs to be preserved, even if it hasn't been recently accessed. Tuning eviction strategies is critical for balancing data retention and memory usage, especially in systems where cache performance must be carefully managed under heavy load.

Another important configuration setting for Redis is the **persistence mode**. Redis supports both **snapshotting (RDB)** and **append-only file (AOF)** persistence options, with different performance trade-offs. By disabling persistence, Redis can run faster since it doesn't need to write data to disk, making it more suitable for purely ephemeral data or when data durability isn't critical. On the other hand, enabling **AOF persistence** can introduce some performance overhead due to the need to persist every write operation, but it guarantees data durability. Tuning the **appendfsync** setting within AOF allows Redis to choose between different frequencies for syncing the file, offering a balance between durability and performance. Additionally, **RDB snapshots** can be scheduled at specific intervals, reducing the I/O impact while providing periodic backups of the dataset.

For **Memcached**, optimizing performance is largely about efficiently managing memory and maximizing throughput. Memcached is a simple, high-performance key-value store designed primarily for caching. One of the first steps in optimizing Memcached is to tune the **memory allocation**. The -m flag allows you to define the maximum amount of memory that Memcached can use. This setting should be carefully adjusted based on the amount of available system memory and the expected size of the cached dataset. Memcached also benefits from setting an appropriate **item size limit** (-I flag) to control the maximum size of individual objects stored in the cache. Larger items can result in increased memory consumption and slower cache access times, so managing the size of objects stored in Memcached is essential for maximizing cache performance.

Another optimization strategy in Memcached involves configuring the **eviction policy**. Memcached uses the **LRU** eviction policy by default, which works well for most caching use cases. However, if your application has specific data patterns, such as frequent changes to a small set of keys, you might consider **sliding expiration** or **time-to-live (TTL)** settings to ensure that older, less frequently used data is removed proactively. Memcached also supports **multithreaded operation**, which is crucial for improving performance on multi-core systems. Enabling multi-threading allows Memcached to handle multiple requests concurrently, leveraging the available CPU resources efficiently. This can significantly reduce response times in environments with high query volumes, ensuring that Memcached remains responsive under heavy load.

For **Apache Ignite**, tuning performance requires understanding the distributed nature of the system and optimizing how data is partitioned and accessed. One of the first things to consider when optimizing Ignite is **memory allocation**. Ignite uses a combination of **off-heap** and **heap memory** to store data, and tuning the memory settings is critical for achieving optimal performance. By storing data **off-heap**, Ignite can avoid the overhead of

Java garbage collection, which can be a significant bottleneck in large-scale distributed systems. The -Xms and -Xmx JVM flags should be adjusted based on the available system memory to ensure that Ignite has sufficient resources to operate effectively without causing excessive paging or garbage collection pauses. In addition to the heap memory settings, Ignite's **memory policies** (such as **on-heap**, **off-heap**, and **direct memory**) allow fine-grained control over how memory is used for caching, ensuring that memory is utilized efficiently without impacting performance.

Ignite's **data partitioning** strategy plays a key role in performance optimization. By default, Ignite uses **consistent hashing** to partition data across nodes in a cluster. This ensures that data is evenly distributed across available nodes, preventing data hotspots and improving scalability. It is important to tune the number of **partitions** based on the dataset's size and the number of nodes in the cluster. Too many partitions can result in excessive metadata overhead, while too few can cause uneven distribution of data and inefficient resource utilization. In addition to partitioning, **affinity** ensures that related data is stored together on the same node, reducing the need for cross-node communication and improving query performance.

Another significant performance optimization for Apache Ignite involves **SQL query optimization**. Ignite allows users to execute SQL queries over distributed data, and tuning query execution plans can greatly improve the system's performance. **Indexes** are one of the most powerful tools for optimizing query performance. By creating indexes on

174

frequently queried columns, Ignite can significantly speed up data retrieval operations. However, index creation comes with a trade-off in memory usage and write performance, so careful consideration should be given to the types of queries being executed and the frequency of data updates. **Query execution plans** in Ignite can also be customized to ensure that queries are executed efficiently across the cluster, minimizing the need for full-table scans and reducing query response times.

Data replication is another key factor to consider in Ignite's performance tuning. While replication provides **fault tolerance** and ensures data availability across nodes, it can also impact write performance due to the need to synchronize data between replicas. Tuning the **replication factor** and **write consistency levels** can help balance the trade-off between performance and reliability. In scenarios where performance is prioritized, it might be beneficial to reduce the replication factor or use **asynchronous replication**, which allows write operations to complete faster at the cost of potentially higher risk during failures.

In all three systems, **monitoring and profiling** are critical components of performance optimization. Tools like **Prometheus**, **Grafana**, and **Datadog** provide real-time metrics on cache hit rates, memory usage, query performance, and other critical factors that affect system performance. By regularly monitoring these metrics, administrators can identify performance bottlenecks, fine-tune configurations, and take proactive steps to resolve issues before they impact users. For example, monitoring the **eviction rates** in Memcached and Redis can help identify whether the cache size is too small, while monitoring **cache miss rates** in Ignite can reveal issues with data partitioning or indexing.

Tuning Redis, Memcached, and Apache Ignite for optimal performance involves understanding the unique characteristics of each system and adjusting configurations to meet the specific needs of the application. Redis excels in scenarios requiring complex data types and real-time messaging, Memcached is ideal for high-throughput, simple key-value caching, and Apache Ignite provides an advanced platform for large-scale, distributed data management and real-time analytics. By optimizing memory management, eviction policies, query execution, and replication strategies, businesses can unlock the full potential of these caching technologies, improving system responsiveness, scalability, and resource efficiency.

Chapter 9: Cache Synchronization and Consistency in Distributed Systems

Cache synchronization and consistency are two critical aspects of managing distributed systems, especially when dealing with multiple caches distributed across several nodes or servers. As applications scale and rely on high-performance caching solutions, maintaining cache consistency becomes vital to ensuring that the data across the system is accurate and up-to-date. In distributed systems, where data is cached on different nodes, cache synchronization ensures that all caches reflect the most recent state of the data, while cache consistency ensures that changes to the data are properly reflected across the system. These concepts become particularly challenging in scenarios where data is frequently updated or invalidated, as maintaining consistency and synchronization without sacrificing performance is complex. For any system designed to leverage caching efficiently, understanding and implementing robust strategies for cache synchronization and consistency is essential for maintaining data integrity and ensuring the system's reliability and performance.

In distributed systems, **cache synchronization** refers to the process of ensuring that all copies of the cached data across various nodes are kept in sync, meaning that any update to a piece of data in one cache must be reflected in the other caches. This is particularly crucial in systems that use **replicated caching**, where multiple copies of the same data are stored on different nodes for fault tolerance and high availability. When a cache is updated, the change needs to be propagated to all other copies of that data in a timely manner. Without proper synchronization, a user could access stale or inconsistent data from different caches, leading to errors, outdated information, and unpredictable behavior in the application.

The simplest approach to cache synchronization is **write-through caching**, where any write operation to the cache is immediately followed by a write to the underlying data store (like a database). This ensures that the cache and the data store are always synchronized, as every change is written to both locations at the same time. However, while write-through caching guarantees synchronization, it can introduce latency, as every write operation requires two steps: one to the cache and another to the data store. Additionally, write-through caching may reduce performance due to the additional disk I/O involved in writing to the data store.

In more complex systems, **write-behind caching** can be used to improve performance. In write-behind, data is written to the cache first, and then asynchronously written to the data store after a certain delay or when the cache reaches a threshold. This allows for faster writes and reduces latency but introduces the risk that the data in the cache may not be immediately consistent with the data in the store, particularly if a failure occurs before the write is propagated to the database. However, this trade-off can be managed with proper failover mechanisms and consistency checks.

Another important technique for cache synchronization is **cache invalidation**. In this approach, when data in the database or the primary data store is modified, the corresponding cache entries are invalidated or refreshed. Cache invalidation ensures that outdated or stale data is removed from the cache, and fresh data is fetched from the data store. Cache invalidation can be **event-driven**, where changes to the data source trigger invalidation messages to be sent to the cache, or it can be **time-based**, where cached data expires after a certain period. Time-to-live (TTL) settings can be used to define how long data remains in the cache before it is considered invalid and removed. The challenge with cache invalidation, however, lies in ensuring that invalidation messages are correctly propagated to all affected caches, particularly in a distributed environment. If the invalidation process is delayed or not executed properly, clients could continue to read stale data from caches.

In distributed systems, **cache consistency** is a broader issue that addresses the correctness of data across the system. Ensuring cache consistency means that all nodes and caches in the system should agree on the current state of data. In a system where data is distributed across multiple caches, **eventual consistency** is often the preferred model. This means that after an update or modification to the data, all caches will eventually be updated to reflect the new data state, but there may be a delay during which some caches contain stale data. Eventual consistency is commonly used in large-scale distributed systems because it allows the system to remain available even during periods of high load or network failures, but it introduces the risk of reading inconsistent data during the period of inconsistency.

For stronger consistency, some systems implement **strong consistency** protocols, which ensure that all caches are updated immediately after a data change is made. Strong consistency provides guarantees that all users will see the most recent version of the data, but it can come with performance overheads, particularly in highly distributed systems with many nodes. Strong consistency protocols can use **two-phase commit (2PC)** or **Paxos** consensus algorithms to ensure that data updates are consistent across nodes. These protocols coordinate with all participating nodes to guarantee that changes to data are propagated correctly, but they introduce additional latency as all nodes need to reach agreement before proceeding with updates.

Distributed cache coherence is another important aspect of cache consistency, particularly when data is partitioned and replicated across multiple nodes. In systems where data is partitioned, consistency between partitions must be managed, ensuring that updates to one partition are reflected in other partitions. **Cache coherence protocols**, such as the **invalidate-based protocol** or the **update-based protocol**, ensure that changes made to data in one partition are propagated to the other partitions to maintain consistency. Cache coherence is especially important in **distributed memory systems** or **distributed databases**, where the data is accessed concurrently by many nodes, and maintaining consistency is critical for ensuring that no conflicting updates are applied.

In more sophisticated setups, **distributed caching frameworks** like **Apache Ignite**, **Redis**, and **Memcached** offer mechanisms for handling cache consistency in distributed systems. Apache Ignite, for example, provides both **partitioned** and **replicated** caches, along with **distributed transactions** to maintain consistency across cache nodes. Ignite's distributed SQL engine ensures that queries across cache partitions are consistent and that the data returned is up-to-date. Redis offers support for **replication** and **pub/sub** features that help with data synchronization across caches, while Memcached provides a simpler but effective model for consistency through **replication** and **eviction policies**.

Another method to enhance cache consistency is the use of **quorum-based** consistency in distributed caches. In a quorum-based system, a write is only considered successful if it has been acknowledged by a majority (or quorum) of the nodes in the system. This ensures that even if some nodes fail or become disconnected, the system can still maintain consistency by relying on the quorum of nodes that have the latest version of the data. Quorum-based consistency reduces the risk of conflicts and ensures that the data seen by clients is consistent, though it may incur additional latency due to the need for coordination between nodes.

Cache synchronization and consistency become especially important when dealing with high-concurrency workloads, where many clients are reading and writing data to the cache simultaneously. In such environments, techniques such as **optimistic concurrency control** and **pessimistic locking** can be used to ensure that race conditions are avoided and that the cache remains in a consistent state even under high load. Optimistic concurrency allows updates to be applied if no conflicts are detected, while pessimistic locking involves locking data for exclusive use to prevent conflicting updates.

Effective cache synchronization and consistency strategies are essential in distributed systems to ensure that data is accurate, available, and up-to-date across all caches in the system. Whether through **cache invalidation**, **eventual consistency**, **strong consistency**, or **distributed cache coherence**, there are various techniques that can be applied based on the needs of the application and the expected data access patterns. By carefully choosing the appropriate approach for maintaining consistency, developers can build distributed systems that handle high throughput, ensure data integrity, and provide fast, reliable access to cached data.

Chapter 10: Real-Time Caching for High-Volume Applications

Real-time caching is a critical component for ensuring high performance and low latency in high-volume applications, where the need for fast data retrieval is paramount. In these applications, users expect immediate responses, and delays due to slow data retrieval from disk-based databases can significantly degrade the user experience. By implementing real-time caching, applications can store frequently accessed data in memory, allowing for rapid retrieval without the need to query the underlying data store, which is often a slower process. High-volume applications, such as e-commerce websites, social media platforms, financial trading systems, and gaming applications, rely on real-time caching to handle the immense load generated by large numbers of concurrent users and high traffic rates. By optimizing data retrieval, real-time caching helps ensure that users can access critical information, such as product details, user profiles, and real-time updates, instantly.

In high-volume applications, data is often queried repeatedly, and caching such data can dramatically improve response times by reducing the need to hit the backend database. For instance, consider an e-commerce site where customers repeatedly view the same set of products during a shopping session. Without caching, each request to view a product would require a query to the database, resulting in unnecessary database load and slower response times. By storing the frequently accessed product data in memory, such as with tools like **Redis** or **Memcached**, subsequent requests to retrieve the product information can be served from the cache, reducing response time to sub-millisecond levels and ensuring a fast user experience.

To handle real-time caching effectively, especially in high-volume environments, the **cache architecture** must be carefully designed to meet the specific needs of the application. One common approach is to use **in-memory data stores**, such as Redis, Memcached, or Apache Ignite, which can store vast amounts of data in RAM, providing the ultra-fast read and write speeds required for real-time applications. These systems are designed to handle high throughput with low latency, which is critical for applications that demand real-time data access. When integrated with distributed systems, these caching platforms can scale horizontally, allowing organizations to add more nodes to the cluster as their data and traffic volumes increase, ensuring that performance remains consistent even under heavy load.

One important consideration for real-time caching in high-volume applications is **data partitioning**. In large-scale distributed systems, the dataset is often too large to fit on a single node, necessitating the distribution of the data across multiple cache nodes. **Data partitioning** divides the data into smaller chunks, known as **partitions**, and distributes these partitions across multiple cache nodes. This enables the system to scale as traffic grows, and allows each cache node to handle a subset of the requests, improving overall system performance. **Sharding**, a form of partitioning, is commonly used in caching systems, particularly for large datasets with a well-defined key space, such as product IDs, user IDs, or session tokens. With **consistent hashing**, distributed caching systems can ensure that data is evenly distributed across the cache nodes, reducing the likelihood of overloading any single node and improving data locality.

Another critical aspect of real-time caching in high-volume systems is managing **cache invalidation** and **eviction**. Cached data can become stale over time or when underlying data changes, and it is essential to have strategies in place for updating or removing outdated data. **Cache invalidation** refers to the process of removing or refreshing cache entries when the underlying data changes. There are various strategies for cache invalidation, including **event-driven invalidation**, where updates to the data store trigger invalidation messages to the cache, and **time-based invalidation**, where cached data is automatically removed after a certain time-to-live (TTL) expires. TTL is commonly used to ensure that cached data is not stored indefinitely, preventing the cache from holding onto outdated information. **Eviction policies**, such as **Least Recently Used (LRU)** or **Least Frequently Used (LFU)**, are employed to manage memory usage in cases where the cache becomes full. These policies ensure that the least relevant or least accessed data is evicted, making space for newer, more frequently requested data.

Cache consistency is another important consideration in high-volume systems. While caching data can improve performance, it also introduces challenges in ensuring that the cached data remains consistent with the source of truth, typically the database. In distributed caching systems, maintaining consistency across multiple nodes can be complex, particularly when data changes frequently. There are two primary consistency models: **strong consistency**, which ensures that all caches are immediately updated whenever data is changed, and **eventual consistency**, where caches are eventually updated but may serve stale data for a brief period. **Eventual consistency** is commonly used in high-volume applications where the absolute accuracy of data at all times is not critical, and where the system must prioritize availability and performance over strict consistency. Tools like **Apache Ignite** provide mechanisms for ensuring that data consistency is maintained across a distributed cache, supporting both **distributed ACID transactions** and **distributed SQL querying**, allowing developers to fine-tune consistency levels based on their specific application needs.

Scalability is another crucial factor when designing a caching layer for high-volume applications. As the number of users grows and more data is generated, the cache layer must be able to scale horizontally to accommodate increasing load. Caching solutions like **Redis Cluster**, **Memcached with sharding**, and **Apache Ignite** support horizontal scaling, allowing additional nodes to be added to the system without significant changes to the application. This means that as traffic increases, new nodes can be added to the cluster, and data can be automatically redistributed to ensure even load distribution. The ability to **auto-scale** in response to fluctuating traffic is vital for applications like e-commerce sites, media streaming platforms, and gaming applications, where user traffic can vary dramatically throughout the day or during special events.

For applications requiring real-time updates, **pub/sub** messaging can be integrated with caching solutions to ensure that cached data is synchronized across nodes. **Redis**, for instance, provides a **publish/subscribe (pub/sub)** mechanism that allows different components of an application to send notifications when data is updated or changed. In a high-volume application, this could be used to broadcast changes to cached data across the system, ensuring that all users or components are immediately notified when new data becomes available or when existing data has been updated. This mechanism ensures that users can access fresh data without waiting for cache expiration, making it particularly useful in scenarios where **live updates** are critical, such as in social media feeds, live sports scores, or financial market data. **Monitoring and analytics** are also key to maintaining cache performance in real-time. Caching systems need to be constantly monitored to track **cache hit rates**, **miss rates**, **latency**, and **memory usage**. Monitoring tools like **Prometheus**, **Grafana**, and **Datadog** allow developers to gain insights into the performance of the caching layer, ensuring that it is operating efficiently and identifying any potential bottlenecks. For example, if a cache miss rate starts to rise, it could indicate that the cache is not storing the right data or that the eviction policy is too aggressive. By integrating monitoring into the caching system, developers can make real-time adjustments to improve performance, optimize memory usage, and ensure the system can handle the required load. Implementing **real-time caching** in high-volume applications requires careful consideration of several factors, including data partitioning, cache invalidation, consistency, scalability, and monitoring. By leveraging the right caching strategies and tools, businesses can ensure that their applications deliver high performance, even as traffic and data volume grow. The combination of **in-memory data stores**, effective **eviction strategies**, **real-time updates**, and **monitoring** ensures that high-volume applications remain fast, reliable, and scalable, meeting the needs of users and the business alike.

Chapter 11: Security and Fault Tolerance in Distributed Caching

Security and fault tolerance are two fundamental concerns when building distributed caching systems, as they play a significant role in ensuring that data is accessible, reliable, and protected from unauthorized access or malicious attacks. In high-performance distributed systems, where caching is used to store critical data and reduce the load on databases, maintaining security and fault tolerance is especially challenging due to the distributed nature of the architecture. Caches are often located across multiple nodes or even geographically dispersed data centers, which increases the attack surface and makes it more difficult to guarantee data integrity and availability. As a result, distributed caching systems must incorporate advanced security measures to safeguard sensitive data and implement robust fault-tolerance mechanisms to maintain availability and consistency, even in the face of failures.

Security in distributed caching systems begins with controlling access to the cache itself. Since caching often stores frequently accessed data, which may include sensitive user information, access control is critical for preventing unauthorized access. Caching solutions such as **Redis**, **Memcached**, and **Apache Ignite** offer several mechanisms for enforcing access control. **Authentication** is the first line of defense, ensuring that only authorized clients or users can connect to the cache. Redis, for example, supports password-based authentication, which can be configured to ensure that only clients with the correct credentials can interact with the cache. Memcached can also be secured by using **SASL (Simple Authentication and Security Layer)**, while Apache Ignite provides a more complex authentication model using **SSL/TLS** certificates and integration with enterprise authentication systems, such as **LDAP** or **Kerberos**. These mechanisms help ensure that only authorized entities can perform operations on the cache, reducing the risk of unauthorized data access.

Beyond authentication, **authorization** is another critical security measure. Authorization determines what actions authenticated users or clients are permitted to perform on the cache. For instance, it may be necessary to restrict certain users from performing cache modifications, while allowing others to perform both read and write operations. In Redis, access control can be enhanced by using **ACLs (Access Control Lists)**, which provide granular control over who can access specific commands, databases, or data structures. Apache Ignite offers role-based access control (RBAC), which allows administrators to define roles with specific privileges. These roles can be assigned to users or clients, ensuring that sensitive data is only accessible by those with the appropriate permissions. By combining authentication with authorization, organizations can ensure that only the right people have access to critical cache data and that any operations on the cache are properly controlled.

Encryption is another essential element of security in distributed caching systems. Since cache data is often stored in memory, it may be exposed to unauthorized parties if appropriate encryption measures are not implemented. **Data-at-rest encryption** ensures that the data stored in the cache is encrypted when saved to disk, preventing unauthorized access to cached data in the event of a physical breach. **Data-in-transit encryption** ensures that data is encrypted while being transmitted between cache nodes or between clients and the cache. Redis and Apache Ignite both support **SSL/TLS** encryption to secure communication between clients and servers, protecting data from eavesdropping or man-in-the-middle attacks. By using strong encryption algorithms, distributed caching systems can protect sensitive data while it is being accessed or stored in memory, significantly improving overall system security.

In addition to data security, **fault tolerance** is a crucial requirement for distributed caching systems. Since caches are often deployed in distributed environments across multiple nodes, ensuring that the system can handle failures without compromising data availability or consistency is essential. Fault tolerance in caching systems is achieved through mechanisms like **replication**, **partitioning**, and **failover**. **Replication** ensures that copies of data are stored across multiple cache nodes. In the event of a node failure, the system can retrieve the data from one of the replicas, ensuring that the cache remains available and that data is not lost. Apache Ignite, for example, supports **data replication** with configurable replication factors, meaning data can be replicated across several nodes in the cluster to ensure availability even if a node fails. **Redis** also supports replication, where one node acts as the master and others as replicas. The replicas can automatically synchronize with the master, ensuring that cache data is available even if the master node goes down.

Another key component of fault tolerance is **partitioning**. Distributed caching systems partition data across multiple nodes to distribute the load and prevent any single node from becoming a bottleneck. **Data partitioning** divides the cache into smaller chunks, with each chunk being stored on a different node in the cluster. If a node fails, the system can still retrieve the data from other nodes that hold the relevant partitions, ensuring that the cache remains operational. **Consistent hashing** is often used to manage data partitioning, as it helps balance the load across the cache nodes and minimizes the data movement required when nodes are added or removed from the cluster. Apache Ignite uses **partitioned** caches, where each cache partition is distributed across nodes, and **partition backups** ensure that data remains available even if a node fails.

Failover mechanisms also play a vital role in ensuring fault tolerance. In distributed systems, failover refers to the automatic switching to a backup node or replica when the primary node becomes unavailable. This is essential in high-availability systems, as it helps minimize downtime and ensures that the application can continue to function even in the event of a failure. Redis supports **automatic failover** using **Redis Sentinel**, which monitors the health of Redis nodes and automatically promotes a replica to master if the primary node goes down. Apache Ignite offers built-in **automatic failover** for its distributed caches, ensuring that if a node fails, its data can be quickly recovered from other nodes in the cluster.

Data consistency is also an important consideration when addressing fault tolerance. In a distributed caching system, it is essential to ensure that data is consistent across all nodes, particularly in environments with high-frequency updates or distributed transactions. Consistency models like **eventual consistency** or **strong consistency** can be implemented depending on the use case. **Eventual consistency** allows data to be updated across nodes asynchronously, ensuring that all replicas eventually converge to the same state. This model is suitable for systems where absolute consistency is not required at all times, such as in caching web page content. **Strong consistency**, on the other hand, ensures that all nodes reflect the most recent write immediately, which is crucial in scenarios like financial transactions or session management. Apache Ignite supports **distributed ACID transactions**, which provide strong consistency guarantees for critical data, while Redis and Memcached typically focus on **eventual consistency** in their distributed cache environments.

To ensure security and fault tolerance, **monitoring** and **alerting** mechanisms are essential for distributed caching systems. These systems need to be continuously monitored for signs of failure, unauthorized access attempts, or performance bottlenecks. Tools like **Prometheus**, **Grafana**, and **Datadog** can be used to monitor key metrics such as memory usage, cache hit/miss rates, node health, and data synchronization across nodes. Setting up alerts based on specific thresholds, such as high cache miss rates or node failures, helps administrators quickly identify and resolve issues before they impact the overall system. By integrating these monitoring tools with automated remediation systems, organizations can ensure that their distributed caching systems remain secure, highly available, and fault-tolerant.

In conclusion, maintaining security and fault tolerance in distributed caching systems involves a combination of strong access controls, encryption, replication, partitioning, failover mechanisms, and monitoring. By implementing these strategies, organizations can build caching systems that are not only high-performing but also resilient and secure, capable of handling failures without compromising data availability or system integrity. These features help ensure that distributed caching solutions remain reliable and safe for applications that require high availability and low latency.

Chapter 12: Monitoring, Troubleshooting, and Scaling Distributed Caching Systems

Monitoring, troubleshooting, and scaling distributed caching systems are essential activities for ensuring that the system performs optimally, remains resilient to failures, and can grow to meet increasing demands. Distributed caching systems, such as **Redis**, **Memcached**, and **Apache Ignite**, are designed to improve application performance by storing frequently accessed data in memory. However, as these systems grow in complexity and scale, it becomes increasingly important to monitor their health, identify issues, and implement solutions to maintain performance and reliability. Effective monitoring helps to detect problems early, allowing administrators to address them before they escalate, while troubleshooting techniques help identify the root causes of performance degradation or system failures. Scaling, on the other hand, ensures that the caching system can handle growing loads by efficiently distributing data across multiple nodes and ensuring that the system remains responsive under high traffic.

Monitoring is the first step in maintaining a distributed caching system. Effective monitoring involves keeping track of a variety of performance metrics and system health indicators, allowing administrators to proactively address potential issues. The most critical metrics for monitoring distributed caching systems include **cache hit/miss ratio**, **latency**, **memory usage**, **CPU usage**, **disk I/O**, **network traffic**, and **node health**. Monitoring the

cache hit/miss ratio helps administrators understand how effective the cache is at serving requests. A high miss rate indicates that the cache is not effectively storing and serving frequently requested data, which could point to an issue with cache size, eviction policies, or data distribution. **Latency**, or the time it takes for the system to respond to requests, is another crucial metric. High latency can result from a variety of issues, such as overloaded nodes, poor data partitioning, or inefficient eviction strategies. By tracking latency, administrators can quickly identify when response times start to degrade and take action.

Memory usage is a critical metric in caching systems because they store data in memory, and if the cache runs out of memory, it can cause data to be evicted too aggressively or, worse, crash the system. Monitoring memory usage helps ensure that the cache is appropriately sized for the workload and can handle peak demand without running out of resources. Similarly, **CPU usage** can help identify performance bottlenecks. High CPU usage might indicate that the system is under heavy load, which could be caused by inefficient queries, excessive cache invalidation, or other issues. **Disk I/O** is another important metric, especially in caching systems like Redis, which support persistence through RDB snapshots or AOF logs. Excessive disk I/O could point to problems with persistence configurations, such as frequent writes to disk, which can slow down system performance.

Network traffic should also be monitored in distributed caching systems, particularly in environments where caches are spread across multiple nodes or data centers. If there is excessive network traffic, it could indicate problems such as **inefficient data replication** or **too many inter-node communications**. Monitoring **node health** is another important aspect of ensuring that the caching system remains operational. If a cache node is down or experiencing high resource usage, it can negatively impact system performance, and its failure may require failover or data replication to ensure continuous operation.

Tools like **Prometheus**, **Grafana**, **Datadog**, and **New Relic** can be integrated with distributed caching systems to collect and visualize performance data. These tools provide dashboards that display real-time and historical data on the system's performance, which helps administrators spot trends, identify potential problems, and take corrective actions. Alerts can be set up to notify administrators when certain thresholds, such as memory usage or latency, exceed predefined limits, enabling rapid response to potential issues.

Once a performance issue is identified through monitoring, the next step is **troubleshooting**. Troubleshooting in distributed caching systems involves identifying the root causes of performance degradation, failures, or inconsistencies. Common problems in distributed caching systems include **cache inconsistency**, **data loss**, **high latency**, and **node failures**. For example, **cache inconsistency** can occur when multiple cache nodes do not synchronize data properly, leading to stale or incorrect data being served to clients. This can be caused by issues with **replication**, **partitioning**, or **cache invalidation** policies. To troubleshoot cache inconsistency, administrators can check the replication status across nodes, verify that the **cache eviction policies** are configured correctly, and ensure that the cache is properly invalidated when data changes in the underlying data store.

Data loss can occur when cache nodes fail or when the system is not configured to persist data correctly. This is especially problematic in systems that rely on in-memory caches for critical data. To troubleshoot data loss, administrators should examine the **persistence settings** (such as RDB snapshots or AOF in Redis) and ensure that they are configured to meet the application's durability requirements. In distributed caching systems, it is also essential to verify that **data replication** is functioning properly, ensuring that data is available on multiple nodes in the event of a node failure. Administrators can check the **replication lag** to determine whether the system is behind in syncing data across nodes.

High latency is another common issue that can be caused by a variety of factors, including overloaded cache nodes, inefficient eviction policies, or poor data partitioning. To troubleshoot high latency, administrators should examine the system's resource usage and check for bottlenecks in the CPU, memory, or network. **Query optimization** and tuning cache eviction policies can also help improve latency by reducing the number of unnecessary cache misses and ensuring that the most frequently accessed data remains in the cache.

Scaling is the process of increasing the system's capacity to handle growing traffic and larger datasets. Scaling a distributed caching system involves **horizontal scaling** (adding more nodes to the system) and **vertical scaling** (increasing the resources of existing nodes). Horizontal scaling is often preferred in distributed caching systems because it allows the system to handle increasing load by distributing the data and workload across more nodes. This helps improve both performance and fault tolerance, as adding nodes provides additional capacity for data storage and processing. **Sharding** or **partitioning** is a technique used to distribute data across nodes, and it is essential for ensuring that the data is balanced and that no node becomes overloaded. In systems like **Redis Cluster** and **Apache Ignite**, data is automatically partitioned across multiple nodes based on a **hashing mechanism**, which helps distribute the load evenly and ensures high availability.

Scaling requires careful management of **data replication** to ensure that data remains consistent and available across nodes. When scaling out a distributed caching system, it's important to ensure that new nodes are added seamlessly without disrupting data access. In Redis, for example, **Redis Sentinel** can be used to automatically manage failover and monitor node health during scaling. Similarly, **Apache Ignite** uses **partitioned** caches to distribute data evenly across nodes and **rebalancing** mechanisms to ensure that data is moved appropriately as new nodes are added.

Another aspect of scaling is the **capacity planning** to ensure that the cache can handle peak load without running out of resources. By analyzing traffic patterns and data access behavior, administrators can predict when scaling will be necessary and plan accordingly. Systems like **Memcached** support dynamic scaling by allowing additional nodes to be added to the system without requiring a major reconfiguration.

In summary, monitoring, troubleshooting, and scaling are key aspects of maintaining distributed caching systems. Monitoring provides real-time insights into system performance, allowing administrators to track critical metrics like cache hit rates, latency, memory usage, and node health. Troubleshooting helps identify the root causes of performance issues or system failures, ensuring that cache consistency, data loss, and latency issues are addressed. Finally, scaling ensures that the caching system can handle growing data and traffic demands by adding nodes and optimizing resource utilization. By leveraging these techniques, organizations can ensure that their distributed caching systems remain fast, reliable, and scalable, even under high load conditions.

Conclusion

In this book, we've explored the essential concepts, tools, and techniques for mastering distributed caching and data management with Redis, Memcached, and Apache Ignite. Each section has provided a deep dive into the fundamentals, advanced strategies, and real-world applications of these powerful technologies, empowering you to build efficient, scalable, and high-performance data systems.

From mastering real-time caching with Redis and Memcached in Book 1, to building robust data systems using Apache Ignite in Book 2, and finally exploring advanced caching techniques in Book 3, you now have the knowledge to design, implement, and optimize distributed caching solutions in any environment.

As data management continues to evolve, the skills you've gained in this book will be critical in tackling the challenges of modern applications, ensuring that your systems are both fast and reliable. Whether you're working with real-time data, complex caching scenarios, or building large-scale, distributed architectures, the insights shared here will serve as a strong foundation for continued growth and success in the world of distributed caching.

Remember, the world of data management is ever-changing. Staying up-to-date with the latest developments in Redis, Memcached, and Apache Ignite will ensure that your systems remain cutting-edge. We encourage you to continue experimenting, learning, and pushing the boundaries of what's possible with distributed caching and data management.

www.ingramcontent.com/pod-product-compliance
Lightning Source LLC
Chambersburg PA
CBHW071245050326
40690CB00011B/2267